ONE COIN
is never enough

WHY AND HOW WE COLLECT

Michael S. Shutty, Jr. Ph.D.

Published by

Krause Publications, a division of F+W Media, Inc.
700 East State Street • Iola, WI 54990-0001
715-445-2214 • 888-457-2873
www.krausebooks.com

To order books or other products call toll-free 1-800-258-0929
or visit us online at www.shopnumismaster.com

ISBN-13: 978-1-4402-1701-2
ISBN-10: 1-4402-1701-7

Cover and Interior Design by Jana Tappa
Edited by Debbie Bradley

Printed in U.S.A.

Dedication

For my wife Wendy, whose unwavering love and support sustained me during many long weekends poking away at the laptop. You have embraced my passion for coins and all the little bits of history that go with them; I know a house littered with the refuse of writing (notepads, photographs, journals, books, and lots of pencils) makes life chaotic, especially when your husband talks incessantly about numismatics and psychology. Yet, I cannot imagine doing any of this without you.

For my father, for whom a quarter is but half a newspaper, I am so touched that you read the entire manuscript and then surprised me by starting discussions about how collectors were different from accumulators and investors. And I will never forget when you implored family members to "read this" as they quickly scattered from the room: It feels good to make you proud.

For my brother, whose thoughtful critique of key chapters led to substantial changes; your keen eye for the storyline kept me grounded. Too bad I cannot get you interested in coins (I tried; I'm sure you remember those Lincoln cents I gave you.), but I am pleased that we share a penchant for abstract studies; for you, it is the siren's call of the chessmen.

For my mother, who unequivocally supports all that I do and boasts about me to others I'll never meet. For years, I coveted that 1838 cent that you found, and recognized as something special, when you were a child playing at the dump. Now you have given it to me. Pitted and dark, this will be the coin that I keep when the others are let go. I also treasure the Buffalo nickels you let me keep during the heady slot-machine afternoons in Japan. I still have every one of them!

Acknowledgments

I want to thank Debbie Bradley, numismatics editorial director at Krause Publications, for her support throughout the process of transforming the manuscript into a book. She was encouraging from the first day that I called, unannounced, trumpeting my book idea. Her ideas for adding a few chapters were instrumental in shaping the direction of the book.

I have learned that creating a book that readers will enjoy from a bundle of ideas on paper is a team effort. I want to thank everyone at Krause who has had a hand in designing the final product.

I want to thank Barbara Gregory, editor-in-chief of *The Numismatist* for publishing a couple of articles that reflected the beginnings of my writing. I want to thank Harry Salyards, editor of *Penny-Wise*, the journal for the Early American Coppers Society, for publishing several articles that also came from my explorations of how and why we collect coins; he has been very complimentary, and I appreciate it.

I also thank David Harper, editor for *Numismatic News*, and Beth Deisher, editor of *Coin World*, for publishing my Viewpoint and Guest Commentary pieces. All of these articles were part of my development as a writer and are important to me.

Special thanks to Heritage Auctions for photos on pages 57 and 75 and to Stack's Auctions for photo on page 79. I want to thank the staff at the American Numismatic Association's Dwight N. Manley Library, as I spent all my free time there during a Summer Seminar a few years ago doing research.

Finally, I want to thank Daniel Sedwick for reinvigorating my collecting in the past few years.

About the Author

Michael S. Shutty, Jr. Ph.D., started collecting Lincoln cents and Buffalo nickels when he was nine years old. He subsequently developed broad ranging interests ranging from Spanish Colonial cobs to early American coppers. He lives with his wife in a 19th-century log house located in the Shenandoah Valley of Virginia where he scours the countryside with a passion for all things antique. He has written articles for *The Numismatist* and *Penny-Wise,* as well as  published a book on vernacular architecture in the Valley. A clinical psychologist by profession, he works at a state psychiatric hospital and holds a teaching appointment at James Madison University.

Table of Contents

Introduction

Why do I collect coins? Am I addicted? Is it some weird substitution for the lack of love in my life? Maybe I am trying to create something. But what am I trying to achieve? Some think of coin collecting as a way to rub up against immortality – the immortality of coins! No, it is probably less noble than all that. Perhaps my interest in coins reflects obsessive-compulsive personality traits: a drive to organize things. Or is it the power that comes with possession? After all, I find a certain pride in owning rare coins; each coin is like a trophy! I want to know what it is that drives this passion of mine. Why do I collect coins?

These musings haunt me – like a hallucination. The voices grow louder with each coin that I acquire. My psychosis became particularly acute when I shelled out hundreds of dollars for a battered Spanish piece of eight.

"Why are you buying this?" they asked.

"What are you going to do with it?"

"Shouldn't you be making another house payment instead?"

But I had to have it. This colonial silver dollar had been recovered from a Spanish galleon that had sunk in 1622! The wooden ship had been torn apart on a coral reef. And this hunk of silver was a piece of the action. Now don't you see? I had to have this piece of eight. Viewing it through a half-inch sheet of glass in some touristy museum would not suffice. I wanted to touch it.

Yet, the voices demanded an answer. Why is it so important? Consequently, I decided to explore my obsession with coins. Not just Spanish pieces of eight, but early American large cents, Buffalo nickels, even State quarters – I collect them all.

As a clinical psychologist who works with folks complaining of obsessions,

A battered Spanish Colonial piece of eight recovered from the Atocha, a galleon that sunk of the Florida Keys in 1622 during a hurricane. This coin was minted between 1598 and 1602 by the strike of a hammer during the reign of Phillip III in Potosi, Bolivia.

compulsions, and even voices, I felt some obligation to come up with some answers. This book is the result. Herein, I explore these nagging questions. It is the only book that specifically examines the act of coin collecting! And guess what? The voices have been reduced to an infrequent whispering – they will never go completely away, just as I will never stop collecting.

My exploration started with the numismatic literature, going back to the first issue of the *American Journal of Numismatics* (1866) and working forward through every journal, magazine, and text I could find. Next, I explored the sociological studies on collecting. Finally, I reviewed my own field: psychological research and theory. But the most important data came from my collecting experiences and those of my brethren. I am in the thick of it: my pockets are full of coins. I live the collecting life.

This book is as much a celebration of coin collecting, as it is an analysis of it. As I delved into my research, I became fascinated by the whole enterprise we call coin collecting. What I found was surprising and unexpected. Yet, it felt deeply familiar – like a *déjà vu* experience.

I believe that we are creating something special when we form coin collections. Our collections are like personal diaries spelled out in objects rather than words. We are storytellers! And what we have to say is important.

It is my aim to invite my dear readers along for the ride. We are all in this together. Our pockets are full of coins! We are fortunate to have such a great hobby. I take special solace in knowing that most, if not all, true collectors understand why I needed that piece of eight.

"And I let my imagination

wander – I was a time traveler.

Isn't this the purpose of magic?"

CHAPTER ONE

My Thousand-Dollar Cent

I purchased a Chain cent at the Baltimore coin show a few years back. The deal happened rather quickly in contrast to the months of acquisition fantasies that came before. The cent was dark and granular – a mosaic of minute corrosive pimples. It was a "chain-only" specimen, and like an impressionist canvas, it had to be admired from 8 inches back to discern the links. Wear softened its bruises, except for a reverse planchet crack between 12 and one. To my eye, the cent had appeal.

Cent collectors know the story well. This lowly cent was struck on a primitive press mounted on a wooden horse in early March of 1793. Burly laborers provided the muscle to heave the horizontal lever forward, propelling the screw in a quick downward twist. Four obverse and two reverse dies, shallowly cut by the inexperienced hand of the engraver, provided the impressions. The coins were substandard from the start: "an exceedingly crude piece of work," one numismatic researcher remarked. The motif was ugly enough to provoke public outcry:

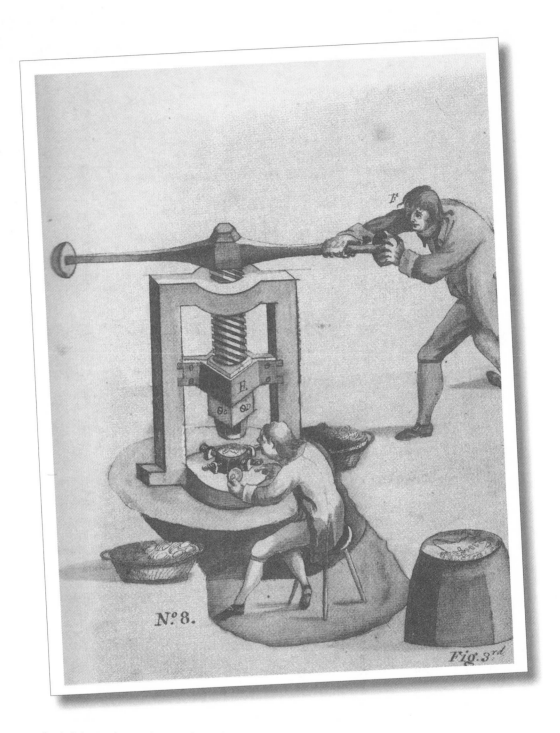

Burly laborers heave the massive weighted lever forward to send the screw downward with enough force to turn planchets into shiny cents.

Liberty "in fright" and "in chains" went the admonition. When the copper blanks were exhausted two weeks later, coining halted. The Chain cent became an anomaly, as a new wreath design was introduced in April.

For 12 months, I had been watching the Chains. Two of the most prolific auction houses offered 55 specimens in the previous year with 15 of these grading between poor and almost good. What a motley lot: not one of them resembled the wonderfully toned red, brown, and yellow darlings – like autumn leaves – that William Sheldon described in his classic reference book *Penny Whimsy*. No, these cents were more akin to dark and mangled leaves heaped at the root.

Prices realized at these auctions accurately captured their individual appeal better than any grading standard. Each design element can be priced *á la carte*: the chain alone brings about $1,000; add a ghost head and a few letters and the price is twice; all this, plus any hint of a date numeral is $3,000. If you can read "1793," the coin sells for $4,000 minimum (unless it is bludgeoned or just too scary to hold).

With this elementary grade/price scheme, I set out on the hunt with the inquiry: "Do you have any Chains in grades poor to almost good?" I boasted a limit of five big ones; but really, I just wanted the chain – *á la carte*! After all, I am a collector of modest means.

Fifteen links is all that is needed to build that mythical bridge to the past that collectors like to talk about. History texts nurture these flights of fancy, as we imagine those early days at the fledging mint on Seventh Street: drafty, dimly lit rooms with few appointments; long hours of physical exertion; a chest of copper blanks along one wall, and a keg of newly minted cents on the other.

The muses of the numismatic historian rouse our imagination, but it is the minted copper in your hand that transports you. You see, Chain cents were there – *in the dimly lit room*. The very room where Washington, Jefferson, and Hamilton cast their shadows: watching the muscled men as they heaved the counterweights of the screw press. There is immediacy to holding a Chain cent that cannot come from historic prose. To experience this kind of magic it does not matter if we rate one coin as *poor* and another as *fine*. All Chain cents were there; they *are* the beginning!

It was a privilege to examine one of these magical vessels up close, to actually touch it at a dealer's table. I was handling an immutable piece of American history. Imagine my shock at the irreverence that some dealers displayed as they plunked their "low-grade" Chain cents down on the glass case (with a sharp slap!) while curtly announcing a "bargain" price. Some used expletive grading terms not typically found in coin guidebooks, as if to belittle them as ugly ducklings. Not all dealers were so graceless; I noticed how one particular dealer gently slid the coin out of its holder, taking time to point out what was there and what was not. His attitude was respectful. It was not a "filler" – but something special.

Chain cents are special because they are survivors from an inauspicious beginning. Centuries of commerce, closets, and collectors have etched their marks in the soft copper. We celebrate, and are humbled by, their durability. Susan Pearce, professor of Museum Studies, put it sharply in her book *Collecting in Contemporary Practice*: "[An object] … which carries meaning is able to do so because unlike ourselves who must die, it bears an "eternal" relationship with the receding past, and it is this that we experience as the power of the actual object."

To possess a Chain cent is to directly control contact with the past. It is a powerful experience that defies rationality. We want to touch the Chain cents like talismans. And we can! This is the power of ownership; this is why viewing one in a museum will never suffice. *It is all about the power to touch it at will.* This is why we collect. Yet, numismatic correctness prevails. Chain cents are to be touched and not touched – it is a power that begets strong, simultaneous approach and avoidance tendencies! Indeed, there is responsibility attached to possession of a Chain cent.

I desperately wanted to feel the contours of the chain with my fingertips. There was very little relief remaining on the coin, and I felt compelled to explore this. As I pondered the urge, I found myself mechanically performing the rituals of numismatic correctness. I consulted a few thick references, examined the cent

Fifteen links is all that is needed to transport you back to the dimly lit coining room of the first United States Mint on a cool day in March 1793.

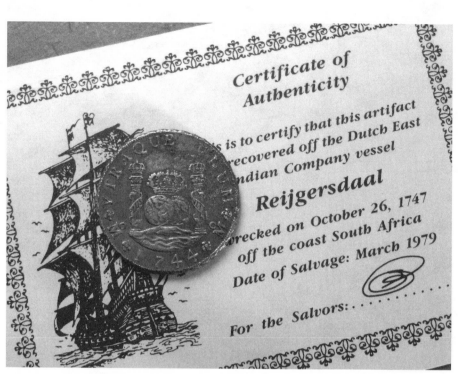

The beginning before the beginning of American Numismatics started with the Spanish Colonial "milled dollar," as our system of dollars and cents was derived from this venerable piece.

with various lenses under different lights, attributed the die variety by discerning the numerals of the fraction despite knowing that some ambiguity would have to suffice.

I carefully brushed it with camel hair and then slipped it into a snug holder. I did not touch the links. Inexplicably, a momentary distraction had derailed the idea (a senior moment perhaps?), and I became engrossed in the above sequence of inclusion activities. Later, I found myself thinking about how the coin had *asserted itself*, relegating me to the well-practiced role of a dutiful curator.

After the coin was secured in its protective holder, the images of the dimly lit room returned. The urge to touch it presented itself again. But the Chain cent was now protected. I relaxed. And I let my imagination wander – I was a time traveler. *Isn't this the purpose of magic?*

Life is frail and fleeting – at my age, seasons go by in a flash. We are challenged at every pause to make sense of it all. Chain cents help us confront these challenges: to understand the world in our own unique way. I think about Henry Voigt, an aging clock mechanic turned die-cutter, making do with few tools while burdened by criticism from others who could not possibly appreciate the hardships faced. This is a tale that I can identify with. It is my story too, and maybe yours.

We all build collections to create a storyline that reflects our view of the world. For me, the Chain cent stands alone amongst many other collecting interests. I am drawn to its humble beginnings in the dimly lit room. Yes, the coin is steeped in history; and yes, maybe George Washington picked this one out of the bin to admire.

But there are reasons deeper than history that shape my relationship with this special coin. To wit, it is a survivor, too worn for serious study, too corroded for an investment – a true collector's coin. It has *all the magic* while still being an everyman's coin!

"Big medicine for a lowly warrior who works 9-to-5 in an office." Is this how I see myself? Perhaps it is. I know that I am not alone, as others will undoubtedly stand in line to have their turn to possess this marvelous Chain cent. But for now, this Chain cent represents all that I love about collecting.

"My search for answers was
personal. ... I had recently
spent a thousand dollars
on a worn-out Chain cent.
I had to know why."

Marvelous Coins

William Sheldon eloquently expressed his attraction toward large cents in the opening pages of *Penny Whimsy*, first published in 1949: "Old copper, like beauty, appears to possess a certain intrinsic quality or charm which for many people is irresistible." He added that there has been a "sustained and almost universal affection shown for the humble copper cent." Sheldon then proceeded to describe the fantasy of all collectors in recounting childhood memories of his father:

> *On evenings when he was feeling especially well disposed, the kitchen lamp would be meticulously trimmed, the red kitchen tablecloth would be cleared of debris and brushed, then out would come the magnifying glass, four or five dog-eared, well-thumbed coin books, and the cigar box with the big cents.*

This is a potent image of the collector: a ritualistic communion with treasured objects. As Sheldon explained, the objective was to "make out the big cents" – to study them and revere them. It was a fascination made all the more enjoyable by the challenges posed by comparison and classification.

Half a century later, this magical time was described anew by large cent specialist Jon Boka, author of the *Provenance Gallery of 1794 Cents*. In the introduction to his book he related:

> *I clear away the assorted and mundane sources of everyday stress which too often clutters my desk, take out a well-worn jeweler's brush, pale green from frequent and gentle copper contact, and switch on the halogen lamp. I then settle in for a brushing and viewing session. These "copper" evenings are especially enjoyable and summon forth a soothing and comfortable sense of wellness.*

It is no coincidence that the passages are similar. The affection for the old coppers forms a bond between the two men that only collectors can truly appreciate. Both Sheldon and Boka marveled at the old copper cents, each uniquely hand-engraved with an aged patina all their own. No two were alike. Every cent had its own wonderful story to tell. Think about it, for a small inanimate object to arouse such emotions is really quite an amazing thing.

Certainly, coins can be alluring. Testimonials claiming that coins have spawned "a collecting life" are not surprising or new. Numismatic historians have often stated that the demise of the large cent in 1857 prompted the start of American numismatics, and that the 50 State quarters program has been responsible for the resurgence of coin collecting today. Coins have magnetism, and many people

Making out the big cents: studying coins and revering
them is one of the greatest joys of numismatics.

T. Harrison Garrett found an odd Horse and Plow copper from New Jersey in his pocket change in the 1860s that led to a life spent collecting. The other coins were just change; perhaps he should have spent them to get a new wallet.

have attributed their decision to begin collecting to their allure.

A lifelong passion for numismatics often starts with a chance encounter. For example, the nearly complete T. Harrison Garrett collection of United States coins was prompted in the 1860s by a colonial coin from New Jersey found in pocket change. It was a serendipitous find that led to 80 years of collecting by the Garrett family. Similarly, the renowned numismatist, Farran Zerbe, began collecting when a bank teller refused to accept a French 50 centimes coin that was inadvertently included in a deposit from his paper delivery route. This unusual coin aroused his curiosity, setting him on a course wherein he collected over 50,000 specimens of United States and world coins that formed the nucleus of the *Chase-Manhattan Bank Money Museum* in New York. Q. David Bowers, perhaps the most prolific numismatic writer of all time, discovered coins when his grandfather gave him an 1893 Columbian half-dollar. Indeed, life-long numismatic passions frequently have had humble beginnings.

How many of us can identify *the coin* that started it all? What is it about these coins? How do they stimulate such intense passions? Is the siren's song of coins that irresistible? To think that seemingly innocuous events such as finding a curious coin in our pocket change can propel us to devote much of our lives to numismatic pursuits is quite amazing!

My search for answers was personal. After all, I had recently spent a thousand dollars on a worn-out Chain cent. I had to know why. Philosophers and social scientists have examined our love affair with objects; surely they would have discovered the allure of coins. What I found surprised me. It was not the coins *per se*. Rather, the coins became special the moment I decided to collect them.

The French philosopher Jean Baudrillard has suggested in *The System of Collecting* that objects can have only two functions. They can be used or possessed. Coins that are spent are known by their function: they are money. In the moment of transaction, they cease to be Washington quarters or Roosevelt dimes. Rather, they are dateless and without variety. We enjoy the things money buys, but pay no attention to the money.

On the other hand, coins that are divested of their function (that is, set aside and collected) take on a symbolic significance that is defined by the collector. No longer pocket change, such coins become *Washington* quarters and *Roosevelt* dimes with meaningful dates and die varieties. They are collectible. We transform them into something special by collecting them.

In my case, the Chain cent was transformed into something special the moment I decided to add it to my collection. Before that, the cent was just an old coin that someone else might collect. Still others would find such an old coin useless, and therefore of no value. But for the collector, the Chain cent offers a wide range of possibilities. For starters, it represents part of a past that fascinates us. In addition, the coin is symbolic in many ways. It represents a keepsake handed down from generations; it represents survivorship against all odds; it represents the culmination of our own coin-hunting saga. In each case, the Chain cent plays a different role as determined by the collector.

This is heavy stuff, but the point is a basic one. We transform coins into marvelous objects when we collect them. The whole enterprise of learning about coins, pursuing them, and finally bringing them home makes them special. As collectors, it is our interest in history, our appreciation of beauty, and our relish for challenge that drives us to assemble collections. For myself, I like to think of it as a gift – a creative bent.

When we elevate pocket change into something special, we imbue coins with certain characteristics. As Susan Pearce explained in her book *Museums, Objects, and Collections*, "Once lifted out of the marketplace … [coins] share a perceived spiritual or intellectual worth and are guarded as such in a way which puts them in a special 'otherworld category.'"

There are four key conditions that characterize each of the coins we have chosen to collect: 1) the coin is singular, 2) the coin demands special care, 3) the coin possesses transcendent properties, and 4) the collecting community exalts the coin.

The coin is singular. Such a coin possesses some superlative quality that makes it desirable beyond its utility as money or bullion. Beauty, rarity, and survivorship all contribute to its unique status. Once collected, a singular coin can be so revered that collectors often think of themselves as temporary custodians. Rare coins are "in residence," not owned. Who can "own" the significance ascribed to them? Instead, we are protectors.

Along these lines, collectors often find kinship with those who cared for the coins before, as Boka described: "Your large cents may have dwelt in the great and legendary collections of the past and will surely pass through many collector generations yet to come."

The coin demands special care. There are explicit and implicit rules for interacting with coins. Numismatic societies and specialist groups provide their members with guides on the care and feeding of coins. The beginner can find a variety of published opinions in the local bookstore about how to protect their coins from the elements – there is even *Coin Collecting for Dummies* by Ron Guth. Moreover, the United States Mint has posted guidelines on its website for safely handling coins. For example, new collectors are instructed: "Don't talk directly over a coin …" and "Hold a coin by its edges, between the thumb and forefinger."

Demands for special care also involve rituals – many of them personal. For example, Boka's copper evenings, where each large cent is carefully "brushed and viewed" in a chronological sequence (1793, 1794, 1795 …) is ceremonial. Such rituals stem from the property of *kratophany*: a power born of simultaneous approach and avoidance tendencies – singular coins are to be touched but not touched. Personal responsibility for the welfare of numismatic treasures weighs heavily here. Cotton gloves, a felt pad and secure holders are required! Hence, rituals govern the kinds of contact allowed, promoting protection and security.

The coin possesses transcendent properties. Transcendence involves the immutable links with history and the awe that accompanies the immortality of objects. Like a "low-tech" time machine, the intimate experience of history *in your hand* is magical. This power to bring history into the present has been recognized by some of the earliest of American collectors, as one observer opined in 1867 issue of the *American Journal of Numismatics*:

> *Every coin or medal of historic interest is a potent talisman: to evoke*
> *the past and people in it with resuscitated life, to secure the present*
> *against oblivion, and give earthly immortality to its heroes. The*
> *owner of a numismatic cabinet is a necromancer and a ruler of the*
> *spirits, and can fill at pleasure, his lonely chamber with shapes of the*
> *departed, and majestic phantasms.*

Indeed, portals to the past are magical. But there is more – much more – as this brand of magic is ultimately an active process. As this observer suggests, the owner is "a ruler of spirits" and has *the power* to call forth "majestic phantasms." Coins are not simply relics that tell us about the past; they stimulate our imagination. As such, coins nurture and shape the collector's experience of history.

Werner Muensterberger, a psychoanalyst who published, *Collecting: An Unruly Passion*, furthered this discussion when he professed that, "people tend to attribute intrinsic power or life substance … to remnants of the past." He further suggested that this power can rub off on us.

Why else do collectors strive to obtain objects associated with powerful figures. Look how they clamor for the possessions of Elvis, Kennedy, or Princess Diana. Certainly, the stewardship of historic coins can be rewarding in a similar way. Herein lies the fascination that unfolds in the serenity of "copper evenings." When we try to "make out the big cents," the coins call out to us and we feel their power.

The collecting community exalts the coin. As the reader is probably well aware, coin collectors are confronted with the irrationality of their pursuits on a regular basis by non-collecting spouses, friends, and associates. Consequently, we form tight social networks of the faithful: from the *American Numismatic Association* to the *Early American Coppers Society*. This creates a social world where certain coins are highly valued. Consequently, the group validates the activities of the coin collector. We need the presence of covetous others to reinforce our faith.

Put another way, an active numismatic marketplace supports our desire to acquire rare and desirable coins – and to spend wads of cash doing it.

It should be clear by now that, as coin collectors, we believe in magic! We love our coins and treat them accordingly no matter how irrational it appears to onlookers. The coins in our collections are special. They have stories to tell, and we marvel at their survivorship, rarity and beauty. Through the act of collecting them, we transform the mundane into the marvelous.

The Numismatist's Dream:

'Twas on a winter evening, beside his cheerful grate,

A numismatist sat at ease, enthroned in a blissful state.

A cabinet beside him, of antique shape, stood nigh,

Stored with those treasures of his heart, the offspring of the die.

Its slides, soft lined with velvet, he drew with careful hand,

And the precious contents, one by one, with loving eye he scanned.

Here lay the coins of nations that rose when Time was young,

The fame of whose achievements has through the ages rung—

Nations whose storied columns lie broken in the dust,

While these their humblest monuments have safe preserved their trust.

—*A.C. Roberts*, American Journal of Numismatics, *March 1870*

"Focusing on a particular

series may be the most

straightforward way to get

started in collecting."

Getting Started:
Collecting a Series

CHAPTER THREE

The urge to collect does not strike suddenly without warning. Rather, numismatic desires creep up on you. A few coins are set aside on the dresser, as the idea percolates. Like a schoolhouse romance, collecting has a desultory start.

Slot machines started me off. Smoky parlors filled with clanking machines were common on Naval bases long after the one-armed bandits had been banned from Main Street. Pressing close to my mother, I scooped out the coins and stacked them. I siphoned off a few nickels here and there (with permission of course) for Cokes. That is when I noticed the Buffaloes.

I stacked them separately, curious to see how many there were. Soon enough, I was actively pursuing them. My fascination with the Buffaloes was noticed and allowed to prosper. I could *keep* them. With an allowance of 50 cents per week (for washing dishes and folding clothes), I could double my take on an afternoon when mom was winning!

The nickels were alluring. They looked ancient and mysterious. The Indian

Chief with his roughhewn features had a dour look that prompted questions. Who was he? And the Buffalo (or Bison) was huge and barely able to squeeze within the rims. Even with an aesthetic honed by comic books, I appreciated that the artistry was radically different from other coins with presidents on them. The old nickels were sculptured with many curious details to discover. Yet, the motifs were at once familiar: a true "Wild West" coin!

The nickels filled a Navy mug in my bedroom. I was becoming a collector; I just did not know it yet. The tipping point for me occurred when I happened on a Buffalo nickel coin folder in a turnstile display next to the *Superman* comics. In an instant, I grasped the significance of the whole enterprise. The dates on the coins became meaningful! And with young inquisitive eyes, I found the mintmarks quickly – a tiny "D" for Denver and an "S" for San Francisco; no mintmark meant Philadelphia.

The coin folder represents *the standard* for coin collectors. It is a holder and guidebook all at once. All the necessary ingredients are there to get started: holes are clearly marked by date and mint, progress toward completion

Buffalo nickels are all-American coins with a rugged design that recalls the Wild West; no wonder young (and old) collectors are attracted to them.

can be judged at a glance, "difficult" coins are labeled by their low mintage figures, and coin preservation is assured by a tight fit.

Most of us who started collecting in grade school began by filling holes in coin folders. These folders were a remarkable innovation when first introduced in the 1930s, as they introduced numismatics to millions of people. The folders prompted children, adults, even families to check pocket change and "fill the holes." Like a bicycle with training wheels, the coin folder included everything needed to begin the trek.

A series of coins defined by a specific design type – like Buffalo nickels – is a beautiful set to behold when completed. But the allure lies in the challenge to complete the set, one coin at a time. Focusing on a particular series may be the most straightforward way to get started in collecting, as the boundaries of the set are clearly defined from the start. With the folder as your guide, the way is clear.

Many collectors relish having such a singular goal. Indeed, set completion is a cardinal feature of coin collecting. Too often, our lives feel burdened with demands that others have chosen for us: work deadlines and honey-do lists come to mind. In contrast, coin collecting is an ambition of our own design. As we have seen, there is something magical about forming sets. By creating them, we transform ordinary objects into something special.

Since each folder has only one spot for every date and mint combination, we can appreciate that each coin plays a unique role in completing the set. This reflects the "no two alike" rule that guides all collecting. There is no place for duplicates, as they do not add to the set. This dilemma is immediately apparent if you are collecting coins from pocket change, as I was in the 1960s with my Buffalo nickels. You will undoubtedly find more than one of a particular date and mint. Typically, the nicest one is chosen and placed in the folder whereas the others are let go.

New collectors should carefully consider what series to collect, as each series provides its own challenges. Of course, this decision may have already happened. We found something interesting and went with it. For me, Buffalo nickels were ruggedly beautiful and reminded me of the Old West I had seen in movies. In addition, they were readily available with medium effort. This mix of aesthetics, images, and challenges was enough to fuel my collecting for over a decade. Other collectors might choose differently, placing more emphasis on the history surrounding a series of coins or the precious metals contained in a folder filled with coins.

Three general guidelines are worth considering when choosing a series to collect. First, it behooves new collectors to explore the wide world of coins to *determine what you like.* Simply checking your pocket change or flipping through a coin magazine in a bookstore can help get a lay of the land. It is not uncommon for beginners to dabble in a few areas before discovering one's true calling. Remember, completing a series can be a long-term commitment, so you want to choose well.

Second, it is important to *select a series that is challenging but not daunting.* Two words apply here: availability and affordability. Collecting cannot happen if there are no coins to be found with reasonable effort and cost. They cannot be too available or cheap either, as the effort of the hunt is an essential component of the hobby. The joy of acquisition is proportional to the efforts put forth in finding and choosing just the "right coin" for the collection. After all, it is the selection process that separates us from those who dump their coins in a Navy mug.

Finally, it is ideal to *find a series that has a manageable level of complexity to keep your interest going.* Minting irregularities, design changes, and historical controversies spice up a series. The more intrigue the better. This is the *crème de la crème* of series collecting: You cultivate a specialty by acquiring this knowledge along the way. We will explore each of these three guidelines for choosing a series to collect.

Determining what you like in a series. Many collectors start with Lincoln cents. They are at once familiar, and old ones with the original Wheat Ear reverse can occasionally be found in pocket change. The portrait of Lincoln is mature and dignified; there is an offset symmetry to the legends and date that is pleasing. The reverse, too, is tidy with two perfectly proportioned Wheat Ears arched along the edges with bold lettering in the center. It is an elegant design that wears

American Eagle 1 ounce bullion coins are extremely popular, as they reprise the Walking Liberty design that graced half dollars from 1916 to 1947 – arguably one of the most beautiful images in all of numismatics.

well. One of the features I have always liked about Lincoln cents is that the date and mintmark are both on the obverse; that way, you can see all the essential information when the coin is placed in the coin folder.

Among the most popular United States coins have been the 50 State quarters series that began in 1999 and ended in 2008. The series was extended in 2009 with the inclusion of five United States territories plus the District of Columbia. These quarters have enjoyed broad appeal for the wide variety of Americana depicted. The parade of new coins continues with the America the Beautiful quarters that began in 2010. Like Lincoln cents, most of these coins can be obtained by thumbing through change at the coffee shop.

If circulated coins seem too pedestrian, the collector can order new ones directly from the United States Mint. In this way, a series of coins can be collected sequentially in real time. Freshly minted coins drip with luster and are without the nicks and scratches that come from cash registers. For some collectors, the challenge is to assemble breathtaking sets of new coins that reflect the pinnacle of minted beauty. In fact, proof-like American Eagle 1 ounce silver bullion coins are one of the hobby's hottest items.

I find it ironic that some of the most beautiful coin designs produced by the United States Mint today are actually resurrections of yesteryear's classic designs. For example, the Walking Liberty design (originally used for half-dollars minted between 1916 and 1947) has been reproduced on the popular 1 ounce silver pieces. The imagery of Ms. Liberty, draped in the American flag, walking confidently toward a rising sun is hard to resist. Even the rugged Buffalo nickel has been recast in gold bullion coins.

As this trend suggests, the lure of the past is inescapable. It is no surprise that advanced collectors gravitate toward obsolete coinage. Besides, two centuries of United States coins are waiting to be discovered. Not everyone will aspire to own a Chain cent of 1793, but many will look back across time and find themselves enamored with the classic designs that once graced United States coinage. Assembling a set of obsolete coins reflects the traditional collecting route; but remember, today's masterworks will be tomorrow's classics – so pick what you like.

How to select a series that is challenging and not daunting. It certainly does not cost much to collect Lincoln cents from circulation – they can be found in parking lots for free! But once you decide to purchase some of the older ones, you will be pleasantly surprised to find that the prices are quite reasonable. Even the first cents from 1909, minted in Philadelphia, can be had in nice condition for five dollars or less. However, early cents from the *Old Granite Lady*, as the San Francisco mint was called, will cost much more.

Collecting guides alert the collector to the nuances of rarity and value; however, it takes hands-on experience to truly appreciate which coins are harder to find in nice condition. Each series contains hard to find (or expensive to buy)

Great numismatic art never dies; the rugged Buffalo nickel was recast in gold and has become one of America's most popular bullion coins.

coins. Seasoned collectors like to call these rare ones the "keys" to completing the collection. Hence, the number of keys in a particular series needs to be considered beforehand when choosing a collecting strategy. Some series have many key coins and are more challenging to complete.

As I hunted Buffalo nickels, I developed a keen sense of which date and mint combinations were available and affordable. Whether comparing slot machine finds or dealer stocks, I gained a deeper, almost intuitive, sense of what was out there. I cultivated these skills by examining hundreds of nickels. My allowance did not go very far, so I learned to purchase carefully. I also learned to act quickly when opportunity knocked.

A low mintage coin is typically a key coin. Sometimes, a high mintage coin can be considered a key coin if only a few nice ones have survived to the present day. Herein lies the complexity of collecting older coins: some coins can be rare all the time; other coins are common in worn conditions, but rarely encountered in nicer grades. Along these lines, the collector needs to consider if the series can be completed within one's budget.

One aspect that is often overlooked when choosing a series to collect is the likeability of circulated coins in a particular series. Like people, some designs wear poorly such that key features are quickly lost causing some coin designs to look stale and ugly. Hence, the collector must consider if moderately worn coins can be tolerated in order to complete the set. Even sets that can be completed with mostly high-grade coins will have a few keys that are prohibitively expensive – for example, 1916-D Mercury dimes in the poor condition will cost about one-thousand dollars!

Finding a series that has a manageable level of complexity to keep your interest going. It is more exciting to collect a series marked by the twists and turns of history. World events like war and economic depression have shaped the quantity and quality of our coinage. Specialized guide books explore these issues and introduce the collector to year-by-year analyses of how a series was produced and changed over time. Consequently, series collecting prompts us to learn about the era in which the coins were used as money. These pursuits are fun, as each tidbit of information makes the coins come alive. Many collectors, like myself, enjoy musing about where our coins were spent and in whose pockets they jingled.

Lincoln cents hold the record for longevity, as they go back to 1909 when Teddy Roosevelt was President. This gives the series a broad historical sweep that few other series can rival. At one time, these cents were the workhorses of domestic commerce. They have survived two world wars, the Roaring '20s, and the Great Depression. These events impacted cent coinage in surprising ways. For example, cents were made from steel in 1943 to save copper that was needed for the war effort. In the subsequent two years, shell casings were recycled to produce cents. In addition, the reverse design was changed several times to celebrate Lincoln's birth. In 1959 the Lincoln Memorial replaced the venerable Wheat Ear design, and 50 years later, in 2009, we had four new designs celebrating Lincoln's life. The Shield reverse was introduced in 2010. All this complexity keeps the collector coming back for more.

As a youngster I was pleased to discover that the design for Buffalo nickels was modified late in the first year of coinage producing two distinct types of 1913 coins. The first type depicted the buffalo standing majestically atop a hill. However, the denomination – "five cents" – was engraved at the base of this mound and was at risk of wearing off rapidly; therefore, the hill was bulldozed and the denomination recessed. Consequently, the buffalo was left standing on a flat prairie – not as dignified a stance, but better for coinage, lest anyone forget that a nickel was worth 5 cents.

Sometimes our own nostalgia can enliven a series. Childhood memories of a simpler time when small change could purchase a world of sweet pleasures are often enough to sustain our interest. I can remember nickel candy bars and packs of Juicy Fruit gum with five sticks for a nickel. Of course I remember one-armed bandits that only swallowed one nickel at a time! These things are all gone, but some of us miss them. Indeed, a series of old coins steeped with nostalgia takes us back time and time again.

It is not surprising that many collectors complete one series and then move to another. Each trek involves a new set of challenges that is met with increased expertise. Series collecting is the mainstay of collecting. It represents a balanced approach to numismatics that blends the history of an era with the history of a particular coin type.

One strategy for expanding to other series is to collect all coins within a chosen denomination. For example, Lincoln cent collectors are likely to move on to Indian cents, as the transition makes intuitive sense (cents!) particularly as the collector is already familiar with the nuances of copper coins. In addition, the colorful history surrounding the use of the lowly cent in commerce is extended back in time like a sequel to a great novel.

Another way to extend a series is to broaden the collection to include coins that circulated within the same era. A popular cadre of coins includes Mercury dimes, Standing Liberty quarters, and Walking Liberty half dollars, as these series all began in 1916. This era of coinage has been dubbed the Renaissance of 20th century coinage since nationally-renown artists were commissioned to design each of the coins. In addition, 1916 was the first year that a different design was used separately for the dime, quarter, and half-dollar.

Series collecting also lends itself to some self-styled variations. One popular way to collect is to form a one-a-year set that ignores mintmarks. An advantage of this approach is that it allows the collector to choose one "best" specimen for each year, thereby skipping over key coins of a particular date and mint combination that are prohibitively expensive or not affordable in pleasing grades. Consequently, the one-a-year set can be completed with higher condition coins.

Another variation goes in the opposite direction where the collector restricts the set to coins from one particular Mint. It may be that the collector wants to collect coins from a local Mint or is interested in the history of a particular Mint. For example, some collectors focus on the Carson City Mint due to its link to the Old West and the silver mines of the Comstock Lode. Also, many of the coins with the fabled "CC" mintmark were produced in low quantities, so rarity is an alluring factor.

A collector who follows the three guidelines described above is likely to find series collecting extremely rewarding. Sure, it requires perseverance and dedication, yet the collector benefits from the well-defined boundaries of the set. A folder completed with carefully chosen coins is quite an accomplishment no matter which series is collected. But the most enduring reward is that the collector has become a specialist.

A good collection is like a well-balanced symphony

orchestra – each item must pass searching inquiry as to its

validity for inclusion, its raison d'étre, and must harmonize

with all the other parts to form an integrated unity. In this

regard no virtuoso piece is a match for the final purpose,

the ensemble, and the complete collection is endowed with

a distinct personality of its own, the possessor of an especial

and perhaps unique beauty or significance.

— *D. Rigby & E. Rigby,* Lock, Stock, and Barrel: The Story of Collecting, 1944

"Keep in mind that the

collector chooses what the

set will be – there are no

firm conventions that must

be followed. "

CHAPTER FOUR

Will the 'Real' Collector Please Stand Up!

As a youngster I diligently searched rolls to fill my Buffalo nickel folder. It was pure amusement motivated solely by the satisfaction of finding the next one. Collecting was simple back then, as one of each date and Mint would suffice. Somewhere along the line, this economy was upset, as I began to acquire duplicates. Perhaps I could save a second one to trade or to sell. Was this the end of innocence? Was I becoming a collector-investor? Or worse yet, was I slipping down the slope toward accumulation?

I think it is important at the outset to consider who is asking these questions. Rarely do you find investors pondering such existential questions; after all, they know the bottom line. And what about accumulators? No, they probably have not thought to ask – in fact, most accumulators do not know they are accumulators until someone (usually a collector) points at them, or their coins, and exclaims, "You are an accumulator!" Clearly, it is the *collectors* who are asking!

It is not surprising that collectors eschew a mentality that hints at accumulation or investment. To treat coins as scrap or as commodities is a punch in the stomach for those of us who relish the satisfaction of finding the next one. Just watch our predictable reaction when confronted with such heresy. We embrace numismatic traditions such as completing sets while publicly professing love for the hobby and devotion to history.

An illustration of this rallying call has been to decry the proliferation of encapsulated coins. I have found this to be a Sisyphean tact to take, as coin prices are soaring and the marketplace is heavily commoditized with "slabs" leading the charge. Everyone has a slab by now. So, have we all lost our innocence? How do we define collecting anyway?

The essence of collecting is acquisition. Each collection begins with the second object, and then a third, and a fourth. This leads to a definition based on numbers: hence, a coffee mug full of Buffalo nickels is on par with a blue Whitman folder of nickels missing only a few of the hard to find San Francisco coins. What distinguishes the two collections is the presence of an acquisition plan in the latter – this collector seeks to obtain one Buffalo nickel of every date and mint combination. The former merely herds them together.

The importance of an acquisition plan is affirmed in nearly all coin collecting guides. The pitfalls of haphazard accumulation are presented with red lights flashing, and this lesson has become the standard protocol for nearly all discussions about starting a collection. In the opening pages of *Coin Collecting for Dummies* by Ron Guth, this requisite discussion is entitled: "Accumulating versus Collecting." This section emphasizes the importance of choosing and developing a collecting specialty. It also acknowledges that coin collectors often start off as accumulators whose curiosity, piqued by a particular specimen, eventually hone their interests.

Harry Rinker, a self-proclaimed collector whose goal is to "buy an antique or collectible every day" and author of, *How To Think Like a Collector*, put it simply: "A sense of having a collection is the key to defining a collection." Hence, it is the judgment of the individual whether or not the accumulation of Buffalo nickels in the mug is a collection or not. But he went further, remarking that, "The true collector never has enough." Put another way: "Continual dissatisfaction is a hallmark of the serious collector." These are astute observations. What he recognized is that collectors are engaged in a continual, active process of acquisition. It is simply not enough for me to possess a folder containing some Buffalo nickels; I must also be actively searching for that 1921-S (a relatively hard-to-find nickel with full details).

Putting these considerations together, sociologist Russell Belk has put forth a comprehensive definition in his book entitled *Collecting in a Consumer Society*. Collecting is defined as: "*A process of actively, selectively, and passionately acquiring and possessing things removed from ordinary use and perceived as part of a set of non-identical objects or experiences.*" This definition adds an emotional aspect to the process suggesting that passion is part of the collecting equation. Also important is the "no two alike" criterion – that is, each object must be different from all the rest.

One way to unravel this academic jumble is to distill *coin collecting* to its core. *Collecting coins is all about forming a set.* This involves defining the boundaries of a series and setting a goal to acquire one example of each. Keep in mind that the collector chooses what the set will be – there are no firm conventions that must be followed. A type set, a date set, a date and mint set, or just coins that the collector finds beautiful fits the criterion. But, a coin added to the collection must interrelate in some meaningful way with all the others. The criterion of "no two alike" is applied such that each coin plays a unique role relevant to the set. Consequently, we can see that *an accumulation* represents the polar opposite of *a collection* on a continuum ranging from "zero set relevance" to "complete set relevance."

Investors are like accumulators because they, too, routinely violate the "no two alike" criterion – *they have more than one!* This upsets the simple economy reflected by the coin folder. And it upsets collectors! I can forgive accumulators, as they often know not what they have. But how many times have you read irate letters in hobby newspapers from collectors bemoaning investors who are

Coin collecting is a passionate pursuit shaped by set completion goals and strict selection criteria governed by the "no two alike" criterion.

driving-up prices and soaking up coins from the bourse? Indeed, investing is only about *salability*!

In order to sort out our feelings on this, I believe it is important to explore how the relationship between accumulators, investors, and collectors has been portrayed in the media. In the following sections, I explore two opposing models popularized by numismatic luminaries Scott Travers and Q. David Bowers. These models capture many of our developmental experiences, as we matured into the "collectors" that we are today. Finally, we explore a comprehensive model that incorporates both viewpoints.

Rational Model

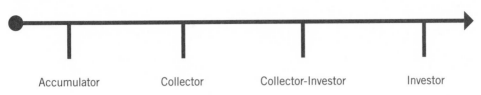

| Accumulator | Collector | Collector-Investor | Investor |

Enjoyment Model

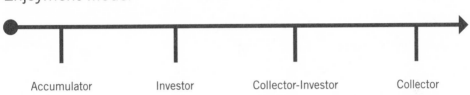

| Accumulator | Investor | Collector-Investor | Collector |

The Rational Model. Scott Travers has outlined a *Rational Model* for understanding the interplay between accumulating, collecting, and investing in his book entitled, *One-Minute Coin Expert.* In his model, a continuum is defined by increasing market-savvy wherein the accumulator marks the lowest end, followed by the true collector, then the collector-investor, with the investor on the high-end pole. Inhabiting the left side of the continuum, Travers described accumulators – with "sugar bowls or jars filled with coins" – as haphazard and without active pursuit. Collectors, on the other hand, zealously seek out coins in a systematic fashion but "with no regard at all to their profit potential." Clearly, these approaches are subjective and capricious at times. In contrast, the highly rational acquisition strategies of the investor-collector, and particularly the investor, place them to the right side of the continuum.

The *Rational Model* is intuitively appealing, as it embodies the familiar developmental progression wherein collectors are viewed as matured accumulators. Curiosity and passion have led them to develop set completion goals. It makes sense that some collectors will take the next step by adopting more rational acquisition strategies, becoming collector-investors (or even investors) in the process. What with rising prices and all the ballyhoo about numismatic investments, it can be difficult to imagine a different outcome. As such, the *Rational Model* reflects a developmental sequence that culminates in the formation of an investor mentality.

The Enjoyment Model. Q. David Bowers has described an alternative perspective in his book *The Expert's Guide to Collecting & Investing in Rare Coins.* He observed that "would-be" accumulators with a passing interest in coins are often prodded into making investment-minded coin purchases via exposure to numismatic marketing hype. In fact, he encourages this developmental path by emphasizing the importance of learning "smart" acquisition strategies prior to opening one's wallet. He outlines these strategies in the opening pages of all his guidebooks; hence, market acumen is put first. With his usual candor, Bowers suggests that "… later you will become fascinated with some of the less obvious, but equally worthwhile, aspects of numismatics." Here, curiosity and passion take hold, but this time, set completion goals follow on the heels of a few well-informed acquisitions, giving rise to a collector-investor mentality.

Bowers' view is best characterized as the *Enjoyment Model*, as he contends that coins will entice you to begin "collecting" whether you start as an accumulator or an investor! Consequently, a developmental trajectory is shaped by the emergence of numismatic passions that follow from an investment strategy. The true collector is not well defined in this model, as Bowers argues that collector-investor dualism is the most rewarding. The *Enjoyment Model* is compelling for its contemporary relevance, recognizing that many collectors today start by purchasing coins from dealers and not by filling coin folders from pocket change. As a result, comparison-shopping has already occurred, exposing them to the market dynamics at the outset.

The Relevance-Salability Model. Since the *Rational* and *Enjoyment Models* suggest two distinct developmental paths, we are still left wondering how to reconcile the two perspectives. A comprehensive model is proposed that recognizes a high-low *relevance* dimension on one axis and a high-low *salability*

The Relevance-Salability Model

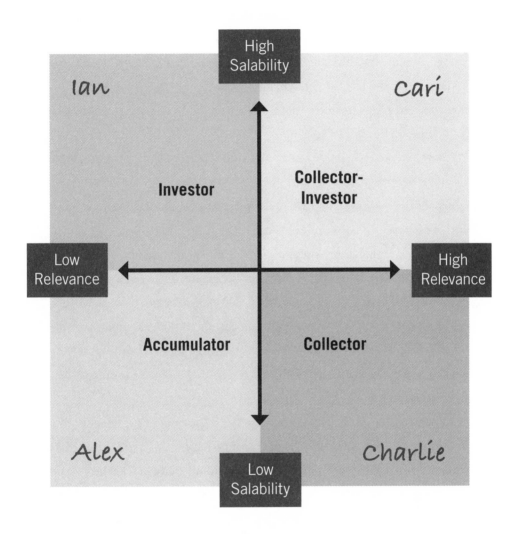

dimension on a perpendicular (or orthogonal) axis to produce four quadrants. Relevance pertains to the role that each coin plays in set completion, whereas salability is all about the profit potential.

This model encompasses both the enjoyment and rational perspectives on a single grid. Starting with the accumulator quadrant, the *Rational Model* is found by moving in a counter-clockwise fashion: Accumulator, Collector, Collector-Investor, and Investor. Alternatively, moving across quadrants in a clockwise fashion depicts the *Enjoyment Model*: Accumulator, Investor, and Collector-Investor. It is unlikely that a collecting life would progress in a diagonal fashion for obvious reasons.

We now explore the characteristics of each quadrant for four individuals with similar-sized wallets.

Consider the hypothetical case of Alex the Accumulator. He amasses coins that strike his fancy in the moment because they are "interesting and unusual" – Buffalo nickels from a television promotion, a few State quarters, a foreign piece, some damaged coins. This assortment possesses little relevance and a modicum of market and/or personal value. A *broad selection process* was used coupled with a *disregard for salability*. His location on the grid could move to the left and downward if he started adding pocket change to his holdings. As such, he could be more of an accumulator depending on how far out on the quadrant he scored.

Next comes Charlie the Collector. He enthusiastically hunts coin shops and shows to fill his Buffalo nickel folder with coins that grade *Very Fine-25* or a bit better. He finds this grade pleasing and within his budget. Charlie will not hesitate to pay more than market price for a fully struck specimen that he needs, as each coin is valued for its role in completing, or upgrading, his set. A *narrow selection process* guided by set completion goals coupled with a *disregard for salability* has shaped his collection. His location on the grid could move to the right and downward if he started systematically adding minute die varieties to his set (that *only* a faithful Buffalo aficionado could appreciate).

In the upper right quadrant, we find Cari the Collector-Investor. She has devoted many hours studying auction records and condition-census estimates for Buffalo nickels. She always buys the best that she can afford and favors encapsulated coins from well-established third-party graders. Despite her goal of completing a date/mint set of Buffalo nickels, Cari often keeps her duplicates for investment when upgrading. She uses a *narrow selection process* guided by set completion goals coupled with a *high regard for salability*. Her location on the grid could move to the right and upward if she started to use her knowledge and experience to cherry-pick underrated coins within her specialty to form a second short-set, and maybe a few triplicates, for investment.

Ian the Investor is considered last. He has charted bid/sell figures and population estimates with the goal of identifying underrated coins that will appreciate in the future. As such, he understands the market dynamics, paying close attention to collecting trends and bullion fluctuations, all with the recognition that high condition grade, fullness of strike, rarity, and popularity are valued features of any numismatic investment. He has several mint-state Buffalo nickels *and* Morgan dollars – all encapsulated by a leading company. Several years ago he purchased some key-date dimes and Lincoln cents, as he forecasted increased collector demand. Ian uses a *mixed selection process*: broad with respect to the types of coins acquired, as set completion goals are absent, yet narrowly defined by his emphasis on salability. His location on the grid could move to the left and upward if he started purchasing more salable coins in bulk.

As this *Relevance-Salability Model* illustrates, patterns of amassing coins is shaped by at least two separate, but intertwined, variables. We can see that the evolution of a collecting life can stem from accumulating or investing. One of the chief lessons that the *Relevance-Salability Model* teaches us is that investing is an orthogonal dimension: it can never be wholly reconciled with collecting. Having more than one will always upset the simple economy of the true collector.

But does the true collector really exist? Sometimes, in the giddy aftermath of filling a hole in our set, we revel with youthful satisfaction of having found the next one. But at other times, we cannot forgo the temptation of using our specialized knowledge to rationally acquire duplicates (or something wholly outside our specialty … eek!) for profit or trade. We may even accumulate some wayward coins along the way! Each acquisition defines us in the moment, nudging us in one direction or another.

Indeed, I have found that my "collecting" defies categorization. One day I am a die-hard collector who just *needs* the coin for the set! The next day I cannot resist the impulse to buy something irrelevant! And yes, I have acquired duplicates, if for no other reason, because they were hard to find the first time around! Have you been there? I am all of the above! I would not have it any other way!

The love of the collector for his chosen subject casts a pleasant aura about all that he says and does in this role. If your interest in this matter should cause you to browse through a half dozen books written by collectors on subjects as diverse as coins, antique rugs, sea shells, autographs, miniatures and china figurines, you would come to recognize a distinctive charm of style, a whimsical good-nature familiar to each, and a uniformly disarming tone of sincerity.

— *D. Rigby & E. Rigby,* Lock, Stock, and Barrel: The Story of Collecting, 1944

"Such are the joys of

collecting coins – knowing

something that few others

know, and finding someone

who, even for a moment,

really wants to hear it!"

CHAPTER FIVE

Connoisseurs and the Others

A few years back a co-worker showed me a Bust half-dollar that was passed down to him. "What can you tell me?" he asked. I carefully tilted the coin toward the light, pointing out the over-date, the metal flow on the star points, and a small die crack along one edge. We had fun squinting to read the rim lettering, as we joked about holding the edge at arm's length to see it up close. As we angled the coin every which way, I could see that he was absolutely fascinated by my description of the *Castaing* machine that applied the rim lettering. For a brief moment, I could feel myself swelling with pride: even my modicum of numismatic trivia was enough to impress. I was jabbering. I felt like a *connoisseur* (even though I only have one Bust half – a rather scudzy one at that). Such are the joys of collecting coins – knowing something that few others know, and finding someone who, even for a moment, really wants to hear it!

Since the Renaissance, collectors have been grouped into two broad categories: *connoisseurs* and *amateurs*. Specialized skills and knowledge define the first group. These skills include assessing authenticity and value, classifying objects, and exercising rational judgment in selecting new additions to the collection. A numismatic connoisseur looking for a mint-state 1807 Bust half dollar would be patient and selective, examining many specimens, before deciding on a purchase. Specific knowledge about the striking characteristics of these large coins and their availability across mint state grades would be called into play. The connoisseur would be able to identify a specimen that is exceptional and undervalued. They would also be willing to wait for another day if no outstanding coins were available.

On the other hand, the *amateur* is typically described as driven by passion and the urgent desire to possess. A decision to acquire is likely to be based upon emotions experienced in the moment. Such a collector would be more apt to purchase the Bust half with the best eye-appeal without a rational analysis of strike or condition grade. The amateur is also more likely to purchase something that day – less willing to wait for a better specimen. Clearly, there is a pejorative taint to this classification scheme with the connoisseur coming out on top. In fact, some descriptions of the amateur suggest that less desirable objects are collected, such as flea market bits and "bric-a-brac."

I find the title of connoisseurship too harsh and unduly biased against budget minded hobbyists like myself. The concept is too narrow to capture the multifarious ways of today's coin collector. A friendlier dichotomy identifies the motives of collectors as either *taxonomic* or *aesthetic*. This scheme is less judgmental and recognizes that skilled collectors find coins appealing in different ways.

The *taxonomic* collector is primarily interested in set completion; therefore, coin selection is based on specialized knowledge about what constitutes a step toward completion. For example, the Bust half dollar collector who is building a set of all 450+ die varieties from 1807 to 1836 will methodically search through stacks of unattributed coins even if well circulated. A battered, low-grade example of a rare variety (perhaps an 1817/4 – only a few known!) will be an exciting find if the collector does not already have one. This Bust half collector is scholarly in his approach, with a reference library of highly specific guidebooks.

In contrast, the *aesthetic* collector does not have a clear idea of when the collection is completed: the lines are drawn and redrawn as the collection grows. New coins are added because of their appeal, extending the breadth of the collection in less predictable ways. Decisions are largely based on curiosity and passion, but the aesthetic collector is not necessarily impulsive. This collector may have specialized knowledge about condition grading and striking characteristics, but is not focused on completing a specific series.

The *aesthetic* collector seeks top rank Bust half dollars and is willing to patiently wait until one is found; worn or battered coins are not considered. In contrast, the *taxonomic* collector would be thrilled to discover a rare die variety – like this well-trodden 1817/4 half – that is essential for completing the set.

In numismatics, it can be difficult to imagine aesthetic collectors, as serial collecting is the norm. Yet the aesthetic collector may begin by selecting a few "very nice" Bust half dollars, extending the set to include some "interesting" varieties as they become available in pleasing grades. Or it could go in some other direction, perhaps Bust half dimes and dimes. Type set collecting provides a reasonable template for the aesthetic collector in numismatics, *but he would only seek out the types that appeal to him.* This collector would probably not be interested in battered, albeit rare, die varieties. Rather, the aesthetic collector has divergent interests: the artwork, the state of preservation, the history of its design – his library is likely to contain a broad smattering of numismatic books.

An intuitive classification of collectors based on *value* has been put forth by Marilynn Karp, author of *In Flagrante Collecto*, wherein she describes three collector types: those with *full pockets*, *deep pockets*, or *big pockets*.

Collectors with *full pockets* are interested in silver, gold, and platinum; they like items of high intrinsic value. Bullion coins and common-date double eagles fill the bill. The caricature for this collector, according to Karp, is the fictional character, Silas Marner: the weaver of Raveloe. He was a gold bug. At the end of the day, he would stack and re-stack his coins, caressing them with his fingers, while admiring their heft. Silas was more speculator than collector. Suffice to say, persons of this ilk highly value, and perhaps are intrigued by, the glint of precious metals.

The collector with *deep pockets* is attracted to items with high extrinsic value. They pursue objects widely recognized as valuable by the collecting fraternity – that is, highly sought after and expensive coins. Flying eagle cents dated 1856 and 1804 silver dollars are for deep pocket collectors. Karp considered Lorenzo de Medici, a real-life Florentine noble whose collecting of classical art was unparalleled during the early Renaissance period, as the template for this type of collector. He especially treasured diminutive objects such as coins, gems, and hard-stone vases. Rarity, high value, and the social status attached to possessing such prized items are the allure for these collectors.

It is the third type of collector, the one with *big pockets*, that Karp says is the "pure" collector, as the items of interest possess neither intrinsic nor extrinsic value. The collector with big pockets is interested in "overlooked material goods that the majority of the population regards with disregard."

Tom Sawyer is the prototype for the big pockets collector. His collection of curious items found consisted of "a key that wouldn't unlock anything, a fragment of chalk, a glass stopper of a decanter, a tin soldier." Collectors of cultural debris, like matchbooks, gum wrappers, and as Karp herself collects – Dixie cup lids from 1930 to 1954 that pictured celebrities – reflect pure collecting. In her opinion, "loving the unloved is the defiled state of collecting from which the motives of all collectors may be deduced."

Of course, coin collectors do not neatly fall into Karp's categories. Yet their general tendencies are captured by her three pocket sizes. For example, many collectors are swayed toward precious metals such that they blend aesthetic desires with the speculative pursuit of high-grade double eagles. Copper and nickel may

Full pockets collecting is all about intrinsic value. Glistening Morgan dollars are irresistible for the collector who wants a "store of value" in every coin.

hold no allure for these full pockets collectors. Alternatively, some collectors may exclusively seek out rarities to form a type set of key coins that appeals to their deep pockets mentality. Finally, numismatic sleuths pursue esoteric (that is, neglected) series of tokens, minute die varieties, and the like for the sheer joy of finding something special – they are the ones with big pockets.

Susan Pearce, writing in *Interpreting Objects and Collections*, has explored collecting strategies to produce a typology that hints at the *underlying dynamics* driving the collecting process: *souvenir collectors, fetishistic collectors*, and *systematic collectors*. As the name implies, their personal associations with objects guide *souvenir* collectors. Collecting enables them to bring parts of their past experiences into the present. The moniker – "memorabilia" – is appropriate to describe the organizing theme in souvenir collections. In this regard, Pearce notes that the collecting process is part of a "nostalgic longing for a past which is seen as better and fuller than a difficult present."

This preoccupation with the past is often included in definitions of coin collecting. Many of us like to romanticize about history. Consequently, nostalgia is extended to a distant time, never directly experienced. For example, Q. David Bowers has done this famously over the course of his writing career. Holding a few Liberty nickels, he reminisces about nickelodeon music boxes, arcades, and theaters buzzing with excitement, as expressed in his series of nostalgia "galleries" in his *Guidebook of Shield and Liberty Head Nickels*.

Fetishistic collectors are passionate. They collect based on their emotional reaction to particular coins. The term "fetish" derives from the psychoanalytic tradition and refers to the process by which an object gains symbolic significance or is held to be mystical in some way. Coins from historic sites are frequently treated this way, much like sacred relics. For example, the two dozen plus Irish coins retrieved at the original Jamestown site in Virginia have been held up as symbolic of the tremendous struggle to survive those early days. Captain John Smith, Powhatan, Pocahontas – these are the images conjured up by such relics. What collector of colonial coins would not treasure these rudely made, and now deteriorated, coppers! And how many collectors have sought out some Irish half

Tom Sawyer's big pockets collection of curious items found represents the purest form of collecting. Devoid of intrinsic or extrinsic worth, these items reflect the innermost motives of the collector.

pennies dated 1601 or 1602 – not from Jamestown *per se* – to forge a connection with this history?

A more straightforward explanation of fetishism in collecting is to recognize its etymology, suggesting an early usage akin to "charm." Fetishistic coin collectors unabashedly exalt their coins. As we have seen, coins are transformed into magical objects when collected. Hence, these emotions are often part of our collecting experience.

Systematic collectors describe most coin collectors given the emphasis placed on completing sets. Whereas souvenir and fetishistic collectors do not necessarily follow strict rules shaping the limits of what is collected, the systematic collector finds purpose in defining and redefining these rules. Numismatics, as a field of study and collecting activity, is defined by series of coins organized by design types, dates and mints, die varieties, and so on. As Pearce notes, "[Systematic] collecting is usually a positive intellectual act designed to demonstrate a point."

A collection of Bust half dollars arranged chronologically by die variety illustrates systematic collecting. The coins tell the story of evolving minting technology, pressures to turn silver bullion into coinage, and commercial practices in the new republic. In short, the material collected shapes the efforts of the systematic collector so that the collection evolves to tell a story. Such collections are most similar to museum exhibits. Clearly, the systematic collector and the taxonomic collector are in the same camp.

Not surprisingly, numismatic writers have joined the fray by proposing several collector typologies. A colorful sorting, based on anecdotal composites, was offered by David Van Meter in his book, *Collecting Coins and Common Sense: A Complete Survival Guide for Today's Collector and Investor.* He identified four types: *elegant collectors, numismatists, specialists, and mass market collectors.*

The *elegant* collector is described as a fashion-conscious, typically well-heeled, individual driven by "a consuming desire for perfection." They are embarked on a "quest for excellence," and coins, like fine art, offer a vehicle for celebrating beauty. Van Meter characterized the tastes of the elegant collectors as guided by the four F's: they seek the *finest* of coins, the most *famous* of coins, the

The bourse floor at ANA, buzzing with curiosity, excitement, and the thrill of the hunt.

coins that *fundamentally* define a historical era or event, and the coins with the *fewest* available. Auction extravaganzas held in prestigious hotels, buzzing with competitive intensity, represent the backdrop for these stylish collectors.

In contrast, the *numismatist* is likely to be found huddled among other enthusiasts around an open dealer's case amidst the din of a crowded coin bourse discussing die varieties and history. As Van Meter emphasized, the scene is one of warmth and mutual support, where dinner plans are made as coins are passed about. For these collectors, the enterprise is "more of a passionate pastime than a pursuit" – a genuine interest in learning about coins and sharing information is predominant. The tastes of the numismatist are guided by the four P's: they seek coins that are *pleasing* with good eye-appeal for the price, *popular* coins that are widely appreciated, coins that are *purchasable* with average budgets such that set completion can be a reasonable goal, and finally coins that are *pertinent* as belonging to the set.

The next type of collector is a trailblazer of sorts, as the *specialist* is driven to leave "the beaten paths of collecting themes … in search of an arcane topic that he can explore, make new discoveries in, and eventually master." As Van Meter summarized, "He adopts the orphans of the numismatic world." Although Van Meter failed to provide four alliterative descriptors, he might have said the specialists seeks coins that are *unusual, undiscovered, underrated,* and *uncontested.* Consequently, the specialist is one who enjoys a challenge and likely has the skills to organize and make sense of a smattering of historical and numismatic research findings that are not yet integrated in any meaningful way.

Finally, the *mass market collector* is described as one with a casual interest in coins who is responsive to market promotions of "round and shiny" and "crusty and old" items that ignite a momentary spark of curiosity. The connotation cannot be missed. This collector is naïve and vulnerable. Here again we have four more P's to guide us, as Van Meter refers to the kinds of coins that are typically chosen by the vendors to promote. They seek coins that are *plentiful,* allow a *profit* to be easily made, are easy to *promote,* and are *pretty* to look at. Coins of the *Old West*; disappearing silver coins that will soon be unavailable; and special-edition gold-plated State quarters – these are the items hawked on late-night television to the masses.

Elegant, taxonomic, fetishistic, specialist, full-deep-big pockets – so what to do with all these characterizations? There is no easy way to combine these typologies. The idea that coin collectors can be cleanly typed is misleading. Coin collectors – in fact, all people – are just too complex. A quick glance about the bourse floor at any large coin show will reveal a diversity of collecting postures that defies attempts to group them in two, three, or even four categories. Some in jeans, a few in suits; some noisily haggling, others laughing and sharing stories; a few nose-deep in well-creased guidebooks while others carry but a scribble pad; some reappearing over and over to take a second look whereas others take a glance and scoop up the whole lot – *coin collectors all.*

How do we make sense of this? One approach is to simply consider the broad traits that collectors show. Personality is defined by two basic characteristics. First, personality consists of traits that are relatively consistent for a given individual over time and circumstance. Secondly, personality accounts for individual differences among people in the same situation. The bourse snapshot given above illustrates the latter, but we can suppose that most collectors behave in a relatively consistent manner from one coin show to the next. We have our patterns. Four *key* personality dimensions come to mind.

First off, curiosity motivates all of us. Most collectors are driven to explore basic numismatic guidebooks and price guides. A few seek out historical sketches of the period in question – wondering when, where, and under what circumstances a particular coin was minted. And fewer still become enchanted, their musings drift far beyond the thick historical texts, stimulating imaginative sojourns. Indeed, these few possess a penchant for daydreaming – a Chain cent becomes a time machine with limitless possibilities. In numismatics, the curiosity factor is probably the most talked about aspect of collecting.

The quest to complete sets is another key factor that characterizes coin collectors. We often think of this as a love of order and control. Adopting a taxonomic approach to collecting wherein each coin is considered as part of a set – this is the collecting life for some. Given the emphasis on serial collecting, it is likely that coins appeal to those who take notice of details, have a knack for categorization, and find "order" soothing. In fact, most of us are busy completing sets. We control our destiny by adhering to specific collecting guidelines that move us toward filling that last hole. Of course, some coin collectors do not appear to be very organized at first glance; their coins are strewed about like the socks of a bachelor. But do not be confused; even these messy hobbyists know what they have and what they are looking for.

The rollercoaster of emotions associated with collecting is another defining factor – namely, collectors relish the hunt. Some thrive on the excitement of the auction floor: a parading succession of coins, anticipation building, frenzied bidding, new sales records! The coin bourse can induce the same buzz, as die varieties await discovery and *wheelin' and dealin'* produces great buys. Here, collecting is defined by the highs and lows of the hunt! Adrenalin is king! It can be a daunting time for some, invigorating for others. At the "quieter" end of the spectrum, the collector may revel in the aftermath of triumph – that is, the solitary enjoyment of examining a new acquisition at home. Here the recipe includes a glass of chardonnay, high-intensity lamp, jeweler's loupe, and some marvelous coins. At this pole, the contentment and relaxation that follows a successful hunt represents the primary emotional experience of enjoying coins.

Finally, many collectors are drawn to the social side of numismatics. Collectors who are active in local clubs and regional numismatic organizations would be rated high on this dimension. Indeed, many collectors believe that the social aspects of numismatics are the most rewarding. Displaying coins, sharing collecting stories, having lively discussions while eating salad and steak is the high point. In contrast, other collectors tend to keep their hobby private, behind closed doors. They like to spend time alone with their coins. Yet, even these collectors are connected to a media network filled with magazines and journals; consequently, they identify themselves as part of a community of numismatists with shared interests and values.

These four dimensions capture much of what is seen on the bourse floor of any large coin show. Can you find your collecting style in these four dimensions? As we have seen, coins are marvelous and magical. We are spellbound, like moths to the light! We are all in active pursuit. Driven by our curiosity, our predilection to organize things, our zeal for the hunt, and our desire to belong to the numismatic community, we collect. I feel fortunate to possess these traits.

In a very real sense, collectors are builders. First, they

lay a solid foundation for their collection, much as a

contractor does when erecting a large building. Then, as

they go forward, they follow a definite plan, much like

an architect's blueprint ... collectors buy coins for their

artistic, cultural, and historical significance ... [and]

are not overly concerned with price, just with having a

particular coin to complete a particular set ... they would

sell their houses or cars or clothing to get that coin.

— *Scott Travers,* The Coin Collector's Survival Manual, 2006

"Buyer's remorse is the

bane of all collectors; lack

of skills and impulsivity

are the usual suspects."

Getting Started: Making out the Grade

CHAPTER SIX

Collectors are drawn to coins smoothed by use. We explore them with child-like curiosity, rubbing them to feel what remains. A thousand hands in as many transactions have come before, leading to this moment. We wax with nostalgia, musing of penny candy, nickel Cokes, and 10-cent comics. Yet, when it comes to our collections, many of us eschew coins tainted by the bold thumbprints of commerce.

We want our coins in the best condition possible – not circulated relics that have been worked. This mindset comes quite naturally from the selection process that is inherent in collecting. We replace our worn coins with better ones as we go along. This process reflects our first awareness of condition grading. Some coins have more details, others a more pleasing color, and a few are inexplicably eye-catching.

I often wonder why the discrepancy. We love the timeworn pieces, but we want newer versions of them. Maybe this is it because *we* want to be the ones to travel back in time. Certainly the numismatic marketplace urges us to buy the best, and so off we go: comparison-shopping. Either way, collectors tend to be obsessed with condition. Just as upgrading forces us to place one coin over another, we tend to judge our collection by how nice our coins look.

A collection composed of high-grade coins is the mark of the connoisseur. Not only does it speak to our keen eye for quality, but it also engenders admiration (and a bit of envy) in others. We like to think that our numismatic finds are newsworthy. Sometimes we become too concerned about condition and value, forgetting why we were so smitten with timeworn coins in the first place.

Nonetheless, learning to determine the quality – that is *the grade* – of a particular coin is of paramount importance. We can be forgiven if we confuse condition grading with value, as hard earned money is involved. In fact, some numismatic pundits assert that grading is the same as pricing, but this is simply not true, as less-than-exceptional coins are frequently offered at high prices. In other words, the coins are over-valued. Furthermore, the specter of "doctored" and counterfeit coins is a real one such that the coin bourse can seem like a minefield for the neophyte. These pitfalls can be a real cause for anxiety among collectors who are simply trying to get a good value.

Imagine attending a big coin show. Like a medieval fair, row upon row of merchants present a dazzling array of goods representing every aspect of numismatics. Collectors flock to the brightly illuminated cases filled with copper, silver, and gold. You are there with your want-list, jeweler's loupe, and a wallet bulging with anticipation. Here is your chance to get a few of the tougher Morgan dollars for your date set.

You move from case to case, row by row. The prices are high, but you forge ahead undaunted. And then you see it: a glossy 1880 Morgan dollar with a broad arc of red-orange toning across the face of Ms. Liberty. The plastic flip has a small red label describing the coin as Mint State-63. You have read about the popularity of toned Morgan dollars, so this appears to be a prime opportunity. Your heart is pounding! You feel the hot breathing of another collector peering over your shoulder, as the dealer offers to "let it go" with a 20 percent discount. Like a gunslinger out of the Old West, you reach for your wallet while deftly slipping your loupe back into your hip pocket after barely a glance.

Like most collectors you excitedly share your "find" in the back of the coin club van as you travel home. The first person points out a small gash in Ms. Liberty's hair shrouded by the deep toning, but now immediately obvious. The second person discovers a carbon spot in the left wing of the eagle, and like any black hole, its gravitational pull draws your eye to it straightaway. The third person is kinder and remarks at how adeptly the coin was cleaned and re-toned; he concludes his analysis with a complement: "It looks natural if you hold it like this" (arm outstretched).

You abruptly tuck the coin away and gaze blankly out the window – shell-shocked. A nightmarish image of a gloved hand dipping your coin into a beaker of orange gook flickers in your head. Disappointment morphs into a gnawing stomach ache. Buyer's remorse is the bane of all collectors; lack of skills and impulsivity are the usual suspects.

This tragedy is replayed at every coin show. Yet folks still show up to audition for the part. A few collectors become so frustrated that they stop collecting altogether. It is a shame that such things happen, as the script can be rewritten with medium effort. In short, collectors need to learn how to assign a condition grade to the coins they are interested in and to understand how this grade reflects value in the marketplace.

Two considerations underscore the need to acquire these skills. First, you want to feel confident that you made a "good buy." No one wants to feel like a dope by paying too much! One of botany's most enduring discoveries is relevant here: *Money does not grow on trees.* Even if you have defined yourself as a true collector who is not concerned with the investment potential of your coins, chances are that you will sleep better at night knowing that someone else would be willing to buy your coins at prices similar to what you paid.

The second consideration is often overlooked: you want to determine exactly what you want in a coin. It defeats the purpose of acquisition if you later realize that the coin is a "space filler" that begs to be upgraded. This form of buyer's remorse is particularly acute when you realize that better specimens could be found with a bit more diligence and a few dollars more. Remember, the goal is to be satisfied with each acquisition with regard for its role in completing the collection. A collection of coins, matched for grade, color, and other chosen qualities is more satisfying. Consequently, condition grading is not just about getting the best deal; it is also about getting what you want.

At its core, condition grading is nothing more than an expert opinion. It is necessarily subjective. When comparing coins, a collector may remark that this one is "good" whereas this other one is "extremely fine" because it has more detail and retains a hint of luster. This is how it was in the early days: inexact adjectives were used to convey an opinion about the overall preservation of a coin. The widely popular *Guidebook of United States Coins* (or *Red Book*) by R. S. Yeoman adopted this format in the late 1940s, labeling coins as "Good, Very Good, Fine, Very Fine, Extra Fine, or Uncirculated."

In 1958, Martin Brown and John Dunn published an innovative book, *A Guide to the Grading of United States Coins*, that provided pen and ink drawings for each grade category across all series of coins. This marked a milestone in the history of condition grading and quickly set the standard in the marketplace. The transition to photographs began with the publication of James Ruddy's *Photograde* in 1970. The format was an instant success and was eventually adopted as the official grading guide by the American Numismatic Association (ANA). All subsequent grading guides have adopted and extended this format. Nowadays, collectors can directly compare their coins with published illustrations and verbal descriptions for each adjectival category.

By the mid-1970s, the call for more precision was addressed by the ANA by assigning numbers ranging from 1 to 70 to the existing adjectival categories. The use of numbers cast an aura of scientific exactitude to the subjective process of grading coins. Many experts were critical of the 70-point system, as it was awkwardly adapted out of convenience from the work of Dr. William Sheldon, who developed this scheme exclusively for grading and valuating large cents in 1949. A base-10 system, ranging between 1 and 100, would have been more sensible.

The matching of adjectives and numbers produced the following grades: Poor-1, Fair-2, Almost Good-3, Good-4, Good-6, Very Good-8, Very Good-10, Fine-12, Fine-15, Very Fine-20, Very Fine-30, Extra Fine-40, Extra Fine-45, Almost Uncirculated-50, Almost Uncirculated-58, and Mint State-60 through Mint State-70. In practice, the use of numbers within each category has been expanded as the marketplace has heated up, so that it is not unusual to see coins graded as G-5 and VF-25. As you can see, this archaic system defies

There are many coin grading guides to choose from; it is recommended that the collector obtain at least two guide books to allow cross referencing.

comprehension much like dividing a mile into eight furlongs (the latter being a measure of how far an ox can pull a plow before resting).

In particular, the hot investment market for Mint State coins has sparked the use of all 11 grades between 60 and 70, including the use of "+" grades by dealers (for example, MS-64+) to indicate that they believe the coin is nearly at the next level, or put another way, is a "high end" coin. This confusing situation has been shaped by the high prices paid for Mint State coins, such that even minor grade differences can translate to significantly greater profits. Consequently, numerical grading has become shorthand for market value and has lost some of it credence in describing a coin's appearance.

As expected, grading criteria has elbowed its way into all introductory collecting guides, often dominating discussions about collecting. The photo comparison format introduced by Ruddy continues to be the preferred mode of instruction, as the photos have become larger and more detailed. Even though the process of condition grading continues to be subjective and imprecise, the chemistry of luster and toning and the delineation of wear patterns have become quite advanced.

A great place to start is the *Official A.N.A. Grading Standards for United States Coins* first published in 1977 and updated every few years thereafter. Another popular book is Beth Deisher's *Making the Grade*. This innovative book uses color-coding superimposed on photographs to identify the highest areas of relief most susceptible to wear for each series of coins. Although the grading guidelines are relatively standardized, it behooves collectors to consult two or more guidebooks to gain a broad perspective of the field and to allow cross-referencing. Yet, book knowledge is only as good as one's ability to use it. It is like learning to swim: a smooth stroke comes from practice in the pool, not memorization of the text. Frankly, most collectors need to swim more!

The task of discerning the difference between grades just a few digits apart (for example, "Good-4" versus "Very Good-8") can be quite challenging! According to the American Numismatic Association's published grading standards, this difference on the Lincoln cent is about half a bowtie on the obverse and two to four lines of the upper grain stalk on the reverse. Discerning these differences on evenly worn cents takes some practice (and young eyes). But remember, most cents are not evenly worn and differ widely with respect to marks and color.

On the other end of the grading continuum, for Mint State coins (such as, "Mint State-60 versus Mint State-64), it often comes down to evaluating subtle variations in luster and determining how blemishes distract from the overall appearance of the coin. Morgan dollars are typically collected in Mint State grades, as collectors look for "choice" specimens with the fewest scratches that come from hitting against other coins in original Mint bags. Some of these "hits" are hidden in the details; others are as obvious as Frankenstein's scar. It takes practice to determine which ones are significant enough to influence condition grades.

It is no surprise that collectors have turned to professional services to grade their coins. These companies have assembled teams of high-profile experts who examine coins for a fee and assign a number grade by consensus. The coins are encapsulated in sealed plastic holders called "slabs" that are labeled with the condition grade and the corporate logo. Business is booming, as slabs have quickly dominated the market for Mint State coins.

The practice of condition grading involves examining the coin up-close in all quadrants and comparing actual wear patterns with the photos published in two or more grading guides.

Of course, the firms compete for your business with a prowess that targets the very soul of collecting. For example, some offer memberships wherein your coins are logged into a database that shows how your coins stack-up to those in "rival" collections. Recognition is given to coins of the highest grade. As might be expected, some firms are touted as more conservative graders than others, underscoring what we all suspected from the start: *even the experts disagree on the grade of a particular coin.* So, how do we really know which coin is the best?

In all the confusion, we are prompted to ask, how does one go about making out the grade? Fortunately, many guidebooks have stepped up to provide straightforward answers to this question. For starters, grading is a determination of how well preserved the coin is from the time it was minted until the present.

Wear or rub is the critical feature that is the foundation of all grading systems. By definition, Mint State coins evidence no wear whatsoever – hence, touching the surface of a newly minted coin can reduce its condition grade by introducing wear. But the touch of a finger is only part of the equation that yields an overall condition grade.

The amount of original mint luster as well as discoloration (or toning) is factored into the condition grade. Collectors highly prize luster. Even a lightly circulated coin is more desirable if it retains some original mint luster. Toning, on the other hand, is a matter of taste: some collectors have an appetite for rainbow toned coins, whereas others vehemently turn away, arguing that toning is nothing more than chemical deterioration. This debate reflects one of the key elements of condition grading: *eye appeal.* Like short-skirts and broad ties, fashions come and go, but they always remain appealing enough to be desirable for some folks.

Professional grading services have assembled teams of experts to examine your coin, assign a consensus grade, and encapsulate it in a tamper-proof plastic "slab" with the condition grade clearly labeled.

What is never desirable is damage. A coin with a hole is shunned. One with a deep cut is better but will attract few buyers unless the coin is extremely rare. Even cleaning is insulting, as the patina of age is removed, leaving an artificial color and surface that is marred beyond repair. In fact, professional graders will not assign a grade to damaged or cleaned coins, as there is no accepted strategy for determining how much of a deduction a scratch or scrubbing deserves.

In addition to damage, repaired – including enhanced – coins are avoided like the plague. Why is this? As before, original surfaces are sacred. But another part of the answer probably reflects the deeply felt fear of being duped. Attempts to pass altered or doctored coins as original have been the subject of lawsuits. Unscrupulous dealers have been known to clean and re-tone coins to give the false impression of a higher grade. Worse yet, some clandestine workshops have re-engraved details to make worn coins seem less so. No collector wants any part of this.

So how does one become proficient at balancing the equation of wear, luster, color, and damage, to determine an overall grade? The short answer is to swim many laps. Once you have identified the coins that you are interested in, you will want to obtain a grading guide that includes a detailed examination of this series. If you like Lincoln cents, then the aforementioned guides will provide you with the basic signposts to look for within each grade. Compare the photos to the descriptions to get a feel for how the coins wear down over time.

The next step is to apply this rudimentary knowledge by looking at many Lincoln cents. A coin bourse or dealer's showroom is the best venue to see many Wheat Ear cents in an afternoon; pocket change will suffice for newer issues. In just a few hours, you will develop a feel for a particular series. You will be surprised at how quickly you are able to discriminate between subtle differences in wear patterns. You will also start to form opinions about which coins are more pleasing than others.

By comparing coins to the grading guide photos you will encounter situations where a particular coin appears to lie in between the grading descriptions. This is not at all unusual; many coins will evidence uneven wear patterns. As you resolve these dilemmas, you will start to develop your own rules for prioritizing specific details and judging grades. In addition, you will find yourself developing preferences about the significance of particular features.

Many of the coins to be evaluated – particularly those in the Mint State grades – will be encapsulated by third-party graders. If you can resist peeking at the grade beforehand, you can check your opinion against those of the experts. This process will allow you to explore different opinions about grading, yielding invaluable market pricing information. It will become apparent that some coins are conservatively graded, whereas others are obviously over-graded. A *good buy* depends on finding the former at reasonable prices.

The methods used to examine coins are relatively straightforward and will become routine with practice. Most guidebooks provide a stepwise procedure to ensure that the coin to be evaluated is safely held, tilted, and rotated so that nothing is missed. Some experts suggest that the coin be inspected one quadrant at a time (that is, upper-left, lower-left, and so on) to insure that all areas are scrutinized. Specific tools are recommended: magnifying loupe, lighting, felt pad underneath to protect against clumsiness. The five general characteristics of condition: wear, luster, color, damage, and eye appeal are discussed thoroughly in most guidebooks. You will develop your own approach, shaped by the series being examined and the grade range of interest.

It is important to remember that the ultimate goal of grading is to acquire coins that represent exactly what you want without feeling like a dope (by paying too much). Beginning collectors often fail to explore what specific design features *they like most* about the series they have chosen to collect. For example, my selection process for circulated Buffalo nickels includes looking for a full horn! Otherwise, the head appears too big and flat – besides, the horn is a defining characteristic of the beast. This is a personal choice. You should make similar choices to enhance your selection process.

This approach has not been lost on seasoned collectors. Full wheat ears (on Lincoln cents), full breast feathers (on Morgan dollars), full bands (on Mercury dimes) and so on represent established signposts of well-struck coins. Yet, these features – and others that are less publicized – are sometimes ignored when formulating a collecting plan, particularly for circulated coins. Even in grades of Fine to Very Fine, the collector can choose coins that are evenly worn and show a certain amount of definition.

One of the advantages of restricting your focus to a particular series is that it will become apparent that there is great variation in the quality of coins produced within a series. In some years, the coins were more flatly struck so that fewer details show in all grades. It might have been the case that coinage demands were high that year, so the minting machinery was set to deliver less pressure, thereby producing lower quality coins. This is important information, as these year-by-

Condition grading is secondary when the coin is extremely rare like this 1737 Higley copper minted in Connecticut; only a handful are known to exist – all of them heavily worn and pitted.

mint differences have to be taken into account when evaluating coins.

Having it your way is perhaps one of the most underrated aspects of what grading is trying to achieve. Harry Salyards, editor of *Penny-Wise*, expressed it this way in the March 1996 issue: "*How do you respond to a coin? Like a concert-goer, do you find yourself drawn in rapt attention, or figuratively squirming in your seat? If the answer is the latter … then pass.*" His message is clear: a coin must please you. Grading is an imprecise metric for a personal aesthetic response.

These arguments can be applied to color and damage too. Lower grade coins vary widely along these dimensions. For instance, large cents minted in the late 1790s are frequently encountered in autumn colors of red, yellow, and green. In addition, many are dented on the edges from being dropped. I know some collectors that cannot tolerate edge bumps but enjoy the autumn colors wrought by corrosion. In contrast, there are other collectors who want their copper to be light brown and smooth even if the edge is bludgeoned.

All told, collectors should look – really look – at the coins. This is where it's at! Do not rely on the grade listed on the "small red label." And do not purchase coins unseen. Rather, look Ms. Liberty in the eye!

*"Indeed, collectors are
curious, thirsty for any
tidbit of fact to weave into
an ever expanding, fanciful,
historic travelogue."*

CHAPTER SEVEN

7

Driven by Curiosity

A few years back I attended a weeklong seminar on early American copper coins. As we were adroitly guided down the path of die variety attribution and condition grading, I began to reflect on how much fun we were having. While the rest of the 9-to-5ers labored to keep the economy going on a Monday morning, here we were – on vacation – working every bit as hard, under hot incandescent lights, thumbing though thick numismatic texts, to decipher minute details on crusty old coins.

Identifying die varieties appears to be a narrowly focused, somewhat obsessive, pursuit at first glance. Consider our tools: flow-chart decision trees, enlarged photos, and magnifiers. Yet, our focus was quite broad! I realized that one reason why these battered old cents invigorated us was that they represented the starting point for a wide-ranging exploration of history, art, and economics. We were embarked on an inductive investigation whose aim was to understand the world we live in. Our instructors knew that the coppers would speak to us in this way; so we spent most of the day examining cents.

Coin collecting is a mental activity of considerable sophistication. Even the most capricious of collectors has to contend with historical, technical, and market information. Weekly and monthly coin publications illustrate the diversity of topics contained under the heading of numismatics. A common format is to profile a particular series of coins by examining every nuance of its design as well as outlining the history of its use. We internalize this information so that dealer inventory lists can elicit the same images, as we ponder how a particular coin can add to our collection.

Consequently, we can study price listings for hours on end to the amazement of our non-collecting friends. The depth of our fascination is made more amazing when we examine the sterile language typical of these price listings: *1794 S-63 DS-2 VG-10 R-3*. What is this cipher? This code translates as follows: Liberty cap large cent, dated 1794, Sheldon variety 63 that pairs obverse 31 [also known

A complicated code is used to describe the 1794 Liberty Cap cent with the "drunken die-cutter's" obverse – also known as the "fallen 4," as the numbers are poorly aligned. Walter Breen speculated that an apprentice, Frederick Riche, who worked for the Mint for only 18 days in June, prepared these faulty dies.

as the "Drunken Diecutter's" or "Fallen 4" obverse] with reverse FF with a rarity rating of 401 to 500 estimated to survive in all grades; on this specimen, the dies have clashed together leaving a slight imprint of the wreath on the temple and chin of Ms. Liberty; the coin is clearly worn, but all details are sharp. Whew! No wonder some think of numismatics as a science.

Yet, thinking about coins prompts a mental process more akin to aesthetics. Our imaginations dilate in flights of historical fantasy. So many of these musings have been published in the numismatic press that the format has become an art form. As one writer explained in the July 1889 *American Journal of Numismatics*:

> *Every coin has its story of human use, could it but speak. It has passed through hands long since reduced to dust, but the coin survives. It has been the purchase price of necessaries and of luxuries, the wages of the laborer and the pay of the soldier. Robbers perhaps have stolen it, perhaps have gained it at the expense of human life. It has been buried around the flag staff on some battle field, or lost in some peril of the traveler, or buried in the earth by some miserly hand whence the rain-wash has exhumed it, or the plough-share, or the spade and pick excavating for a foundation wall. What incidents could any ancient piece add to the history of ages had an audible voice been given to it! Possibly it fell from the hand of an Emperor, as he scattered his gifts on his coronation day; perhaps it was the last stake of some gamester, by which he sought to recover his wasted fortune.*

Here lies the allure of coin collecting. Our coins allow us to tell marvelous stories. The more we know about them, the more interesting the storylines. Indeed, collectors are curious, thirsty for any tidbit of fact to weave into an ever expanding, fanciful, historic travelogue.

Simply put, *curiosity* is a desire to know and learn. *Interest* refers to the experience of curiosity. There is a vast literature to suggest that under optimal conditions, we are motivated to learn. This vitality is normative, not exceptional. This is what I observed during the early American copper seminar. As we counted leaves and berries to decipher which die variety, I surveyed our classroom: everyone, from 13 to 60 years of age, diligently working, hour after hour, motivated by the sheer pleasure of "making out the big cents."

Daniel Berlyne, a social psychologist, provided the seminal analysis of curiosity in his book, *Conflict, Arousal, and Curiosity*, published in the 1960s. Despite the passage of time, most researchers still agree on its core elements. According to Berlyne, curiosity is aroused by two variables that shape our responses to objects. These variables are *novelty* and *complexity*.

Novel coins create tension because they demand a creative response. For example, a State quarter never seen before is likely to spark interest enough to examine it closely and make some attempt to decipher how the design reflects the state heritage. This takes extra effort. In the end, one is rewarded with a deeper appreciation of the quarter and the state.

For this process to occur, the coin must be different enough to attract attention, but similar enough so that it is understandable with medium effort. Just about everyone knows that new State quarters were issued each year from 1999 to 2008. New designs were anticipated. However, if a coin is too discrepant – that is, lies far outside daily experience – then it may only get a passing glance or be avoided. For example, a Presidential dollar coin will certainly get noticed, but may be rejected: "I'll take the paper bill, thank you." We are more accustomed to examining our quarters; dollar coins are not familiar, so we do not look at them long enough. Of course, it all depends on each person's experiences, as some may find dollar coins interesting.

Complexity involves the demands inherent in understanding the coins we are familiar with. For example, Morgan dollars are popular and available in large quantities; many die varieties have been identified that add a layer of complexity to the series. Yet some collectors find these varieties uninteresting. Like novelty, there is a distinct relationship: too little or too much complexity fails to arouse curiosity. But when design differences are understood with medium effort, then curiosity is stimulated. For Morgan dollars, the eagle tail-feather varieties of 1878 (the first year of issue) add moderate complexity, as these design differences are included in most guidebooks. Hence, collectors typically want them – they

Strong remnants of the underlying eight tail feathers can be seen poking out from the eagle's plumage on this 1878 Morgan dollar from the Philadelphia Mint. This die variety is one of the strongest examples of 15 modified dies used early in that year. Since the variety is listed in the *Red Book*, many collectors start exploring the nuances of the Morgan series by counting tail feathers on 1878 dollars.

appreciate that these tail-feather varieties reflect the Mint's efforts to improve the striking of these robust coins.

Perhaps the best example of widely accepted complexity in numismatics is the 1909 Lincoln cent with the designers initials – VDB – placed (too) prominently on the reverse. Public outcry that the initials were promoting Victor D. Brenner prompted the Mint to remove the initials after only a few weeks of minting. These events created a rarity for those coins minted at San Francisco. But more importantly, it stimulated intense interest then, and today, as these VDB cents have all the makings of a good story: a new design, perceived self-promotion, public outcry, and a quick removal of the offending letters, resulting in a rarity. Just the right amount of complexity has produced enough excitement to last a century.

The Guide Book of United States Coins (or *Red Book*) provides an excellent illustration of what design types have been found interesting over the years. Both the 1909 VDB Lincoln cents and the 1878 Morgan dollar tail-feather varieties are prominently listed and illustrated. In fact, many collectors start out managing novelty and complexity by limiting their pursuits to those varieties listed in the *Red Book*. Hence, our sustained interest in coins stems from the particular qualities of the coins themselves coupled with our collecting experiences. Sometimes changing circumstances, like the retirement of a coin design, sparks our curiosity by increasing novelty and complexity all at once. As familiar coins become less available, they become more interesting.

It is no wonder that collecting in the United States has been energized by the start or discontinuation of coin designs. The demise of the large cent, the introduction of the 5-cent nickels, and most recently, the start of the *50 State quarters* program provide clear examples. In contrast, the reason why some obsolete coins have been unloved by mainstream collectors is due to their complete unfamiliarity (that is, their high novelty and complexity). Odd denomination coins such as 3-cent and 20-cent pieces, and to a lesser extent, copper half-cents fall into this category. No one seems to like the Susan B. Anthony dollars either,

Unfamiliar, unloved, and uncollected dollar coins of today; when was the last time you have seen one?

as they are just too strange! How many serious collectors of these series do you know?

Studies in art appreciation have suggested that both an appraisal of the novelty and complexity of art *plus* an appraisal of one's ability to understand the art are associated with interest. It is a two-step process: first, novelty and complexity are appraised; and second, one's ability to understand the object is appraised. Surprise turns to interest when the collector is prepared for the challenge. Such discoveries feel so good that we want to experience them over and over again. Hence, we are motivated to learn and explore new collecting possibilities with a zeal rarely found in other pursuits. Consequently, our ability to appreciate increasing levels of novelty and complexity push many of us to specialize. This is a deeply gratifying process, as our enjoyment increases at each step.

This progression can be seen in the Morgan dollar collector considered earlier. The collector may begin the journey into the realm of die varieties by first considering the first year hub varieties: the seven, eight, and seven over eight tail-feather varieties. This may prompt reading about the design changes made in those early months of 1878. Before long before this collector begins to notice other major hub varieties such as old-style 1878 reverse dies used in Carson City two years later. Next, it will be the major overdates of 1880. A spark of novelty-

---

"I will see you a dollar and raise you a dollar." Just knowing that silver dollars were heavily used in places like New Orleans and Carson City is exciting – this is fun information and we "like" having it. In contrast, we "need" market information about our silver dollars, and we feel anxious when we do not have it.

complexity is met with more knowledge at each step of the way.

Curiosity has a dual nature. Sometimes new knowledge is simply enjoyed, as the process of discovering new information feels good. Many numismatic facts are superfluous, yet fun to learn. As we have seen, facts fuel the imagination. This kind of information was not missed beforehand, but brings a smile when encountered unexpectedly. For example, to learn that Morgan dollars circulated freely in New Orleans and on the western frontier is fascinating and rewarding for its ability to conjure up images of how these cartwheels were used in daily transactions. This kind of information is "liked" and actively sought for the enjoyment it brings.

On the other hand, new knowledge can be pursued from a sense of deprivation. There is an urgent demand for the information. Numismatic market projections are often of this ilk. Prior to acquiring a Morgan dollar condition graded as Mint State (MS)-65, the collector "requires" knowledge about condition rarity and current value in order to negotiate a purchase. There is a "need to know" feeling about these statistics. As such, the collector may experience anxiety about this information gap. This kind of information is "wanted" and sought to provide *peace of mind.*

Collectors often become obsessed with wanted information in a competitive marketplace. For example, specific knowledge about a coin's valuation is given a high priority, as it is considered to be essential information. In contrast, knowing that poker players on Bourbon Street favored silver dollars in the 1880s is not afforded high priority status. The critical difference between liking and wanting is that wanting is associated with negative feelings when the information is not immediately available. Ask any collector who has stretched her budget to acquire a rarity: there is often anxiety about the authenticity and current market value of such a coin. Alternatively, liked information is not missed. This is unfortunate, as liked information is more strongly related to enjoyment.

As with many things in life, our curiosity waxes and wanes. Our newest acquisitions simply become less interesting over time, as they are examined once and again. That is to say, the coins eventually become familiar. The higher complexity of some coins sustains interest longer, but this too is a linear process whereby interest declines over time and exposure. Coin collectors maintain interest in their coins by increasing complexity via historical study, die variety attribution, and on-going comparison with other specimens. Following the numismatic market may also sustain interest. Eventually our interest is overshadowed by our desire for new acquisitions.

Curiosity is stimulated anew by adding to the collection. A new coin often initiates a round of comparison. In this way, interest in the whole collection is invigorated. This is an enjoyable process, as it is based on the skills of the collector. Reviewing a collection that is well cataloged, taking note of each die variety to ensure the accuracy of the attribution recorded on the label, is an intensely enjoyable process wherein a host of numismatic skills are brought into play. Generally speaking, *interest stems from the characteristics inherent in a particular coin; enjoyment comes from the skills of the collector.*

Consequently, enjoyment increases as the collector matures. Each new acquisition redefines the collection while boosting the skills of the collector. For example, the fortunate acquisition of a sharply struck Morgan dollar may prompt the collector to consider upgrading several other pieces. Similarly, the addition of an overdate variety may prompt the search for more. As such, the collection is dynamic: novelty and complexity are introduced and re-introduced as the collection grows. Furthermore, as new collecting guides and historical sketches are published, the collector is likely to take a second look at all coins in the collection. Collecting, then, involves an ever-changing canvas with regular infusions of novelty and complexity that are met with increased expertise and enjoyment.

Collecting can stall however. Interest and enjoyment wanes. *Collector fatigue* takes hold. This crisis in collecting is described by C. Saeman in the November 1961 *The Numismatist*:

> *Suppose one finally fills his board. Perhaps after awhile the monotony of seeing so many pieces exactly alike except for dates and mint marks may not furnish enough allurement to stimulate and hold his interest. This may be a critical period for his hobby. The ardor and enthusiasm with which he started may have cooled, and he is satisfied in believing he has reached his goal. He may decide to keep what he has but makes no further effort to explore the many additional attractive phases of his hobby.*

Collecting fatigue among seasoned collectors is usually only temporary. Loss of interest and a dampening of motivation are common to all pursuits. Sometimes a completed set produces a lull wherein a new collecting focus must be decided on. A crisis can arise as the collection nears completion and only the expensive rarities remain. In this case, interest clashes with a limited budget and collecting fatigue develops. In other scenarios, the desired coins are simply not available in the marketplace and fatigue is borne out of frustration. Finally, as in all things, a long and unwinding road can lead to boredom. One begins to tire of the same old features: full feathers, full horns, full steps, full bell lines, and the like.

Most collectors survive fatigue and are better for it. If interest and curiosity depend upon a sustained, incoming stream of novel and complex information (and coins), then research and diversity is part of the cure. We have also seen that enjoyment depends on continued skill building. In January 1963, Charles Johnson shared his views on this topic in *The Numismatist*:

> *Study and research prevents us from tiring of our collections. The mere act of collecting and possessing coins cannot satisfy a thinking mind. After casual examination, coins in themselves are uninteresting. Something more is needed. Thus, as we endeavor to understand the legends, designs, varieties and background of our coins and paper money, we acquire a tremendous amount of knowledge in many related fields. Frequently a numismatic collection supplies the motive and springboard for an enjoyable study of many phases of history, art, economics, politics, money, banking and other associated subjects.*

These suggestions shape the template for most numismatic periodicals whose articles in any given month may span all the disciplines named above. This broad network of associations underscores the important role that coins can play in our quest for information about the world we live in. Suffice to say, coin collectors are curious company!

Although the shells have similar characteristics, a particular one will possess a unique feature which catches my attention, and I stoop down to collect. I question its origin and ask who else might have held it. I muse that I didn't start the beach walk with collecting in mind, but what has caught my eye has to touch my hand. I wonder if the two are connected, if one is the reflex reaction of the other – and so it continues until the vacation is ended. Medals and coins offer for me the similar experiences, both visual and tactile. Unlike the shells, they are made by man and tell of his art and history. They reveal the whole sea of civilization.

— Cory Gillilland, *Curator of the National Numismatic Collection,*
quoted in Q. David Bowers, The Numismatist's Downtown Companion, 1994

"It is during the heat of the

moment, when the hunt

is clearly on, that we may

experience our greatest

enjoyment."

Treasure Hunting

Which is sweeter: hitting the bourse floor searching for that special coin or actually nabbing it? This is a question I have often asked myself. I suspect most collectors would heartily endorse the latter. Acquiring the "perfect" coin *is* the sweetest experience! After all, isn't this what collecting is about? I want a 1796 Draped Bust cent, and I want it now!

But what about coin hunting? Certainly, there is no better time to be had than having a wad of cash and cruising from one dealer to another with all that potential energy. When I really think about it, I have spent more time searching for a nice girl with a 96 tagged to her robe than any other collecting activity. In fact, I have enjoyed the hunt.

This singular focus is what I crave in life. Many of us are likely to have a tired list of vaguely defined goals (lose some weight, choose some better stocks, take a closer look at the car because it needs something).

But it sure is nice to have one very specific goal: in this case, get the girl! But

Let the hunt begin! Rows of coins promise to contain a few rarities or under-graded specimens to be "cherry-picked." The thrill of the hunt is an essential part of coin collecting, and even if we suspect that these coins have been picked over, we want to take a look for ourselves!

maybe there is something gained in the wanting.

A convincing argument can be made that the hunt is the most fundamental aspect of collecting. It is through the zealous pursuit of coins that we unequivocally assert ourselves as collectors. The hunting metaphor was aptly expressed over a century ago in the *American Journal of Numismatics* (February 1867) when one observer quipped, "the numismatist follows the scent of a rare coin as a hound does that of a rabbit, and is never satisfied till he has traced it to its burrow."

The hunting metaphor is firmly embedded in our numismatic folklore. Old-timers reminiscing about the "early days" when a 1909-S VDB could be had by

That's what they all say: unsearched Lincoln cents with a few "S" mints thrown in! But we want to believe, so we try our luck at finding that special coin.

Who could resist looking through this jar of Grandma's coins? The fantasy of the great find burns in all collectors, as the thrill of discovery is an indelible part of collecting.

searching pocket change represent an enduring segment of the hobby literature. I wish I had collected back then. In this day and age, die variety hunting offers the same opportunities. Maybe I will be the next one to discover a previously unknown variety of a 1796 cent. Indeed, coin collecting has often been equated with treasure hunting.

Popular coin guides – with titles such as, *Strike it Rich with Pocket Change*, and *How to Make Money in Coins Right Now* – highlight that our numismatic expertise will be rewarded. Treasure is being found everywhere! For example, with the introduction of the presidential dollar coins in February 2007, a dramatic series of rare minting errors occurred due to quality control problems associated with the new lettered-edge design. As a result, the edges were left blank on an estimated 55,000 George Washington coins. This was followed by similar errors on the John Adams and Thomas Jefferson issues. Collectors scrambled to find these rarities worth their weight in gold. In fact, plain-edge Jefferson dollars (MS-64) were valued at $2,000 at the start of 2011.

The drama of discovering treasure has been replayed over and over again in the form of "cherry picking." The term refers to a process of using specialized knowledge to select undervalued, yet highly desirable coins. "Cherry picking" forms the core of most modern day treasure fantasies. The anticipation of the *great find* burns in the hearts of all collectors. As Scott Travers, author of *The Coin Collector's Survival Manual*, commented, "There's something deeply satisfying about picking up a bargain – in coins as in anything else – by outsmarting somebody else, particularly when that somebody is supposed to be an expert on the subject."

The hunt must be challenging to be satisfying. I want to find the 1796 cent on my own. To be given the coin as a gift would dilute the pleasure. Rather, it is the anticipation and prolonged effort that sweetens the experience. Rigby and Rigby put it bluntly, extending the hunting metaphor in *Lock, Stock, and Barrel: A Story of Collecting*:

> *The true collector is a transformed hunter. Although his hands are seldom bloodstained, his intense concentration, like the hunter's, is pointed toward the objective of getting a full bag. There is the same patient following of clues, the same wile and guile, the matching of wits and the pitting of strengths, the tense expectation as the pursuit nears its completion, the deep exultation following a triumph.*

In this light, the once hunted and now found coin is like a trophy. I can imagine holding up my Draped Bust cent in triumph, celebrating my prowess as a hunter!

Numismatic auctions offer a prime opportunity to observe the drama of the hunt. It is in this highly competitive arena that intense passion plays are perpetrated for the world to see. Bidding represents the culmination of a prolonged build-up of acquisition fantasies that started weeks before. We are enticed by glossy catalogs filled with tantalizing photos and pedigrees: who can resist such game? The excitement extends to hundreds of living rooms where Internet bidders vie to win! Competition is part of the hunt: each coin goes home with one elated collector, and the rest are disappointed!

William King provided one of the best descriptions of the emotional whirlwind that is coin hunting in his book *Collections of Nothing*:

> *Collectors all know the joyful and terrifying moment of glimpsing a new and wonderful object for the collection. Eyes lock on the prey, and the breathing deepens. Instantly, we size up the whole context in which the object appears and assess the hazards. We do that to make the crucial calculation of how to acquire, all other questions now peripheral.*

For me, spotting the cent of my dreams in an auction catalog has gone this way: Who else wants it? How high will it go? What is my strategy? How can I win? Gosh! Hunting feels much like courtship.

It is not surprising that auctions make it easy for bidders to let emotions overrule reason – busting budgets! Auction fever or mania is common parlance for exuberance. As a result, most collector guides caution potential bidders to set, or at least consider, a monetary limit prior to entering the fray. Of course, some collectors bid with abandon, as in the case of J. R. Frankenfield (described by Ron Guth in *Coin Collecting for Dummies*): "… [bidding] on the extremely rare 1795 Sheldon-79 Large Cent,

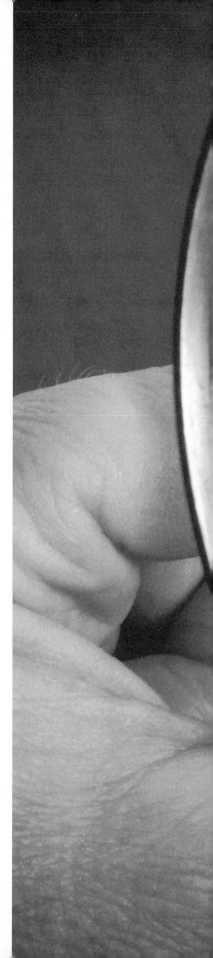

Flow occurs when your field of vision narrows and all your energies become focused on the coin in front of you. These are the best of times, when we slip away and become oblivious to the outside world.

he taped his bidder card to the wall and left it there until he finally won the lot for over $100,000, setting a record price for the variety." For him, winning the coin was all that mattered.

It is during the heat of the moment, when the hunt is clearly on, that we may experience our greatest enjoyment. At this point, some collectors can be characterized as motivated solely by desire. It is a rare moment in life to be so free! Mihaly Csikszentmihalyi, a psychologist and author of several books on peak experiences, has labeled such moments as "flow" experiences.

Flow involves the feeling of effortless action that is smooth, efficient, and pleasurable. I relish those times when I am moving about the bourse floor looking at all the girls of 1796 – not a care in the world intrudes; it is just the Draped Busts and me. This is flow! I am totally absorbed in my copper cent universe. For others, frenzied auction bidding can lead to flow – akin to the sheer excitement of a roller coaster. Still others experience flow when immersed in deep numismatic discussions. It feels extraordinary when we are on top of our game and wholly absorbed without distraction. These moments are recalled as the best of times. *Flow is about peak experiences that we produce!*

The experience of flow has two defining ingredients. First, flow occurs in situations that prompt us to muster all our skills to meet the challenges of the task. We must strike a balance between our abilities and the demands of the situation. Coin collecting calls forth many skills – condition grading, attribution of die varieties, and market savvy – just to name a few. Being competitive in the auction gallery or on the bourse floor requires a strategic execution of these skills. Making all the right moves feels great and is part of the flow experience.

The second ingredient of flow has to do with the merging of action and awareness such that they become one. When we examine a coin for our collection, the totality of our experience is focused on the coin in front of us. We are oblivious to the outside world as all extraneous information is blocked out. For an instant, we are not concerned about our budget, or the need for a stronger loupe, or our insecurities about grading. Paradoxically, we are not even aware of how much fun we are having.

When I talk to the girls of 1796, time slips away during these moments, such that hours pass as minutes. This distortion of time is characteristic of flow. I am engrossed with each cent, as if I was drawn into a parallel universe where life revolves around the coins in my hand. Indeed, many collectors will tell you that an afternoon on the bourse floor can pass in a flash! Next thing you know it is 5 o'clock; you are hypoglycemic and exhausted.

It is important to note a distinction at this point: *Flow differs from relaxation.* Whereas flow involves a balance of challenge and skills, relaxation involves situations when the demands are relatively low. Relaxation is more restorative

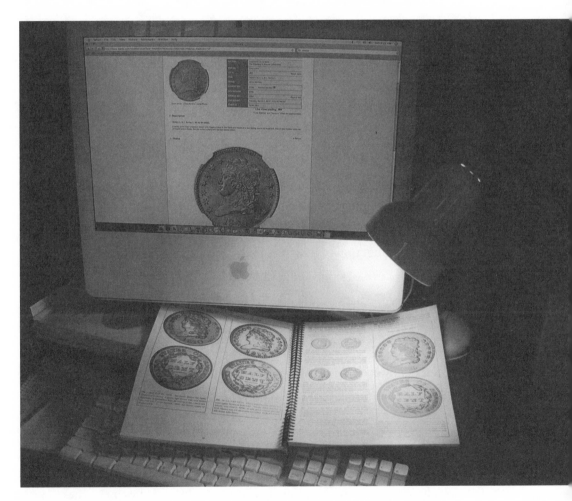

High-tech coin hunting allows the excitement of the auction to be brought into the living room!

than exhilarating. Some collectors define numismatic bliss by the relaxation it provides – that is, they find the restorative aspects most rewarding. It could be argued that these folks find acquisition sweeter than hunting.

The calmer side of collecting has much to commend it. An evening of reviewing one's holdings, or reading about history, can be a nourishing activity. For some collectors, these are the defining moments of one's numismatic quest. The advantages of these quieter moments are described in the following passage published in the April 1943 *The Numismatist*, amidst the Second World War:

> *The collector who can now and then dismiss from his mind the turmoil that has invaded our lives, and spend a satisfying hour with the treasures he has accumulated over the years, can very definitely realize that restful and stabilizing experience. He will need imagination to carry him varying distances into the past, and some knowledge and appreciation to interpret what he finds there; but given these, "the cares that infest the day" are for the time being forgotten.*

The ingredients necessary – an hour's time, imagination, and knowledge – to escape the tremor in the world, are clearly spelled out.

On balance, we can appreciate that coin collecting occurs in a cycle of tension-building and tension-release. The often frenetic and emotionally charged atmosphere of the auction or bourse is followed by quieter moments when the collector slips away to the den to further examine the new acquisitions. In this regard, it seems that the process of collecting perpetuates this topsy-turvy pattern. It is difficult to have one without the other. On the surface, this drama appears to be driven by our desire for closure. We want to have them all, and *then* we will relax. However, this viewpoint is fraught with inconsistency. We cannot relax; if we did, we would cease to be collectors! As we shall see, completion of the collection jeopardizes the whole enterprise!

Collections are often defined by what is missing. When I lay out my Draped Bust cents to take stock, I become vexed. It is immediately clear that I do not have the 1796. I realize that my collection is defined, not by what lies on the desk in front of me, but by what is not there. The significance of this vacancy cannot be overlooked. I know you have been there, as nearly all collectors – in the course of proudly showing their collection – will remark about what is missing and the plans they have to obtain one.

We are acutely aware of the empty holes in our folders or the "scudzy" specimen in need of an upgrade. The missing coin reflects our competence to shape and define the collection. We recognize when an important specimen is needed for completion. In addition, the missing coin acquires special status simply by

Missing coins set the stage for tracking and hunting while stimulating hours of acquisition fantasies.

being absent, invigorating the hunt and setting up high expectations for our satisfaction once the coin is found. Since rare coins are often the ones missing, these expectations are heightened even more, as only a few can aspire to own one.

Striving for closure is really about keeping the hunt alive. John Wright, author of *The Cent Book: 1816-1839*, offered this commentary about why he chose to study die varieties as a strategy to prolong the hunt:

> *With a broad enough specialty I could guarantee that I would never again suffer the total letdown of the "completed collection syndrome" that always crept in shortly after plugging that last hole of each album. The fun is in the CHASE, in the TREASURE HUNT, in the SEEKING – "NOT" in the HAVING. Why do you think active collectors sell their coins soon after plugging that last hole? So I resolved to chase vigorously, to learn all I could, and to enjoy every mile of the road.*

Consequently, collectors experience ambivalence as closure nears. We want to complete the set, but we are afraid to. To the extent that "collecting" is part of our identity, we must ask: What happens when there is nothing left to collect? What are you then? If I finally nab that 1796 cent, what do I do next? Will I be left without a soul? Probably not, as I always find a new goal: a demure sweetheart with 1804 embroidered on her chest comes to mind. Like me, most collectors strive for closure, while ensuring that they never get there.

When the collection approaches completion, the rules for closure are cleverly redefined so that more coins can be added. And the process repeats. In this way, the collector creates tension and releases it again. This is the emotional life of the collector: hunting, acquiring, and then hunting anew. The excitement can be intense, and the relaxation is nurturing (and much needed). Peak experiences of flow occur throughout. And so the drama continues. Actual completion is not the goal of the collecting life – as Sigmund Freud once said, "A collection to which there are no new additions is really dead." At least in collecting, we have the power to ensure that we never have to have a final experience.

A truly successful and dramatic auction will follow the pattern of a stage play. In the first act there's a burst of excitement as the players are all introduced. In the second act, the characters reveal their strengths and weaknesses as the plot, driven by the conflict over the prize, is crystallized. Everyone in the audience knows that Act III will bring a resolution. Just as someone always gets the girl in a romance, someone always gets the coin at an auction. Of course the play, and the auction, will be all the more satisfying and exciting if the ending comes with a surprising twist.

— *Bruce McNall with Michael D'Antonio,* Fun While it Lasted:
My Rise and Fall in the Land of Fame and Fortune, 2003

"What is it about die varieties that intrigues us so? Numismatic observers have pondered this question for over a century."

Getting Started:
Variety is the
Spice of Collecting

CHAPTER NINE

A funny thing happened one summer night in 1955. Much to the chagrin of the quality-control officials, a dramatic blooper escaped detection at the Philadelphia Mint. The date and lettering was boldly doubled on the Lincoln cents; you could not look at one without rubbing your eyes.

The hub used to form the obverse die had rotated a few degrees between impressions creating this out of focus anomaly. Mint reports suggested that the error was discovered after the die had produced 40,000 cents. Since half of these were mixed in with those from normal dies, the coiner decided to release them. Who would notice such a small variation? *Just about everyone!*

A feverish hunt ensued, as collectors rushed to search bankrolls of cents. Lucky finds were reported in Massachusetts and upstate New York. Many of the doubled die cents were discovered in cigarette packs that sold for 23 cents when purchased from vending machines since it was customary to place two new pennies in the cellophane packaging to provide change for a quarter. The doubled die was definitely worth looking for, as the price quickly rose to over $10 in just a few months!

The 1955 doubled die cent has all the hallmarks of a great variety. It is so obviously blundered, and the story of its origin tells just enough about the coining process to make stimulating dinner conversation. In addition, nice specimens are not so rare to be unavailable; yet, today's $1,000 price tag for "fine" examples make them exclusive. These factors earned the 1955 blooper the distinction of being listed in the *Guide Book of United States Coins* (*Red Book*) by R. S. Yeoman.

The adventures of Lincoln cent collecting were just revving up however, as another major variety emerged in 1960 that sparked a similar furor – at least among collectors. In the spring of that year it was reported that the date numerals had been enlarged to extend the life of the dies. Even though the modification was slight, eagle-eyed collectors quickly honed in on the difference. The fire was

The 1955 doubled-die Lincoln cent represents the best that die varieties have to offer: obvious punch-drunk doubling, rarity, and an all too human story of tired Mint workers who underestimated public scrutiny.

stoked even more when it was discovered that some small date dies were re-impressed by the large date hub to produce a large over small date variety!

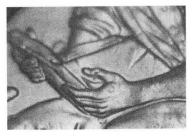

The saga of cent varieties has continued into the present day, as eagle-eyed collectors have discovered six fingers on Lincoln's left hand. This is what makes variety collecting so much fun: everyone has the opportunity to discover something new!

Still intoxicated by the remarkable ascent of the 1955 doubled die that came before, speculators amassed the 1960 small date coins from both the Philadelphia and Denver mints. Prices soared despite the large quantities that were available. Once the dust settled, the coins were recognized as quite common with several million examples produced. Nonetheless, the die variety had created enough hoopla to be listed in the *Red Book,* further popularizing the idea that valuable die varieties could be found in pocket change.

Flashing forward to just a few years back, several varieties of 2009 "Formative Years" cents with doubled fingers on Lincoln's hand were discovered within weeks after their release. Although these were only minor anomalies that primarily appeal to die-hard cent specialists, they brought excitement to the series. Indeed, hunting for die varieties represents the next logical step for collectors who have chosen to specialize in a series.

The opportunity to play the role of numismatic pioneer is irresistible. New discoveries are publicized weekly in the numismatic press; even minute variations between dies have ignited enthusiastic discussion. To meet the demand for cataloging all these discoveries, the two-volume set entitled, *The Cherry-Pickers Guide to Rare Die Varieties,* by Bill Fivaz and J. T. Stanton has led the way by providing high-resolution photographs of each anomaly. This has become essential reading for the three-eyed specialist.

What is it about die varieties that intrigues us so? Numismatic observers have pondered this question for over a century. In 1877 an anonymous author wrote in the *American Journal of Numismatics* that collectors had "run mad" with the search for "cracked dies, large and small dates, straight and oblique numeral

"My, what big cheeks you have!" Over-zealous use of the chisel by the die engraver, Robert Scot, produced this popular die variety appropriately named "Apple Cheeks" by William Sheldon's father.

characters, thick and thin planchets, over-struck dates, &c., &c., which seem to me, in my ignorance, to be a direct perversion of the higher and more aesthetic objects of numismatic science." Some 70 years later, the debate continued, as another writer pondered in the July 1940 issue of *The Numismatist* whether or not "ferreting out some minute die-break or irregularity" is really numismatics?

Despite these detractors, the history of numismatics clearly underscores the excitement that comes with reaching deeper and deeper within the rims of the coin. Certainly, exclusivity is part of the equation. All collectors want their coins to stand out from the rest. By definition, a notable die variety is more rare that a nondescript coin. In addition, the attribution of a specific die variety requires that the collector be savvy enough to appreciate the difference – it is the prodigious mark of the specialist. Finally, die varieties level the playing field among collectors, as it allows those with specialized knowledge to cherry-pick rare coins despite having fewer bucks to spend. No wonder we love what we see through our magnifying glass!

It is important to understand the difference between a die variety and a striking error. Die varieties involve specific characteristics of a working die used to produce coins. All the coins struck from a particular die will show the same characteristics. Hence, all 1955 doubled die cents are identical, as each one came from the same obverse die. In contrast, error coins show doubled impressions due to mechanical problems during striking. If the ejection mechanism jams, the planchet can be struck twice. In this case, the double struck coin is unique, as once the machinery becomes unstuck, the coins produced are normal again.

Die varieties themselves can be produced either intentionally or in error. For example, the 1955 doubled-die cent was clearly an error, as the hub rotated unexpectedly when the working die was produced. If the quality control inspectors were wearing their glasses, they would have recognized the magnitude of the error and destroyed the die. In contrast, the 1960 small-date cents represent a design element that was discontinued after a few months in favor of a better design. Both small and large date cents were made intentionally.

The distinction between intentional and error die varieties is not always clear, as deliberate changes to the working die were often blundered by unsteady hands, poor vision and miscalculation. During the first decades of the United States Mint, working dies were routinely finished by hand; consequently, every die was unique despite best efforts to make them identical. Since the working dies were too valuable to discard if a mistake was made, the engraver would re-work the die with a small chisel until it was suitable for use. Engravers frequently "touched up" worn or damaged dies in this way, perhaps giving Ms. Liberty a new hairdo in the process – *an extra curl if you please.*

Collectors of 1794 large cents relish these differences, as over 56 die varieties (listed by Sheldon numbers: S-17 to S-72) have been identified. Each variety is defined by the pairing of a particular obverse die with a particular reverse die. This potpourri of re-cut dates, embellished hairlines, and facials has captivated early copper collectors for decades and has provided impetus for some of the most colorful descriptions in numismatics. For example, mint engraver Robert Scot, once scooped his chisel too deep endowing Ms. Liberty with protruding cheeks to produce the die variety affectionately known as the "Apple Cheeks" cent. This slip of the hand is not technically in error, but she sure does not look like her sisters.

When we step back and survey the entire field of die varieties, it should not be surprising that over-dates rank among the most popular anomalies across all series of coins. After all, collectors working on date and mint sets are apt to focus their gaze on the numerals before anything else. Fortunately for the die variety enthusiasts, mint engravers put forth considerable effort to update the dies when the calendar year ran out; consequently, there are many over-dates to choose from. Typically, the last digit (or two) would be ground down and a new digit was punched over top; the old number invariably peeked out from under the new one similar to a partially erased arithmetic error – herein lies all the excitement!

One of the most fertile areas for over-date hunting is within the Bust half-dollar series: there are over 15 different over-date varieties spanning the 1807 to 1839 series with only a couple of extreme rarities. The 1880 over 79 varieties in the Morgan dollar series are also extremely popular, as there are over ten of

The 8 over low 7 is one of the most dramatic 1880-CC over-date varieties, as the crossbar of the 7 can be seen diagonally within the first loop of the second 8, and the stem of the 7 boldly protrudes below. Like a partially-erased arithmetic error, over-dates immediately attract attention.

these over-dates with none of them outside the reach of the average collector. Of course, the large cents have many over-dates to choose from as well. As we have seen, these coins spark our curiosity, prompting many date and mint collectors to extend their sets to include these unusual pieces.

Modern series, too, have their share of over-dates. The demands for coinage during two World Wars provided the background for some of the greatest rarities of the 20th century. Close to my own heart is the 1918/7-D Buffalo nickel with the crossbar of a 7 boldly asserting itself from behind the 8. This one is rare with an estimated population of less than 100,000. A similar event occurred for 1918/7-S Standing Liberty quarters; another rare coin made all the more difficult by the tendency for dates to be worn off after only a few years of circulation.

The tumultuous period of the Second World War produced an over-date among 5-cent coins with some 1943 Jefferson nickels showing a 3 over 2; this one is harder to see but is relatively inexpensive and available. Some of these nickels might still be circulating or be found in a dealer's showcase without being attributed. Finally, the 1942 Mercury dimes from both Philadelphia and Denver show bold 2 over 1 over-dates of moderate rarity. All of these modern over-dates are listed in the *Red Book* and are considered by many to be part of the series.

In addition to over-dates, there is a broad spectrum of date anomalies that stem from poor alignment of the punch when making the die by hand. Careless or rushed engravers have been known to punch digits (and letters) upside-down or grossly crooked; the error is usually corrected, but as before, the aberrant figure shows through much to the delight of collectors. These varieties have occurred in nearly all series prior to 1900 and are relatively common so that no collector has to go without.

In a similar fashion, mintmarks were individually punched into the die until the early 1990s; consequently, many mistakes were made well into the modern era. The whole field of mintmark variations (known as RPMs: re-punched mintmarks) is ripe for exploration, as new varieties among pre-1990 coins are still being discovered. In addition, over-mintmarks – where a D has been punched over an S or vice versa – are known for most contemporary series. Certainly, mintmark variations represent a collecting specialty that can be pursued by searching pocket change.

Some die varieties such as die cracks are progressive and stretch the distinction between die varieties and minting errors. As working dies age, they become worn and cracked; consequently, the coins will reflect this deterioration. For example, a small crack on the die will appear as a raised, jagged ridge on the coin's surface. When the crack gets larger, the ridge will be bolder. If a piece of the die chips out or become recessed, this will appear as a small blob on the coin – called a "cud." Like wrinkles on a weathered face, the life history of the die is revealed by its cracks and cuds.

Some collectors have specialized in progressive die breaks, classifying coins from the same die according to "die states" defined by distinct stages of die deterioration. This is perhaps the most advanced form of die variety collecting.

Collectors of early series – like large cents – use this information to determine how long a typical die lasted in those formative years. These collectors are pushing the limits of series collecting to scholarly heights, as each sequence of die states reveals more and more about the intricate details of what happened in the dimly lit coining room.

A few dramatic cases of die breakdown have captured popular imagination, achieving the status of being listed in the *Red Book*. The 1922 "plain" cent is one such issue where the die was damaged and subsequently grinded (or lapped) smooth and greased such that the "D" mintmark disappeared over time. Since dates and mintmarks are critical to series collectors, this anomaly was initially confused as a Philadelphia issue, except that only Denver minted cents in 1922. Consequently, this coin became highly sought after and attained a much higher status relative to other *ground-down* coins. Yet, one detractor opined in the May 1945 *The Numismatist*: "Collectors who feel that they 'must' own a 1922 cent with an obliterated mintmark should use a tack-hammer on the mintmark of a well-struck specimen." Some unscrupulous individuals have done just that and have tried to pass them off as the real thing: *caveat emptor*.

Another illustrious die variety caused by overzealous grinding is the "three-legged" 1937-D Buffalo nickel. As before, the die was lapped to repair a defect, this time erasing the right foreleg of the beast. It should be obvious by now that it does not take much elbow grease to smooth it all away. The oddity caught on since the leg was so neatly removed – besides, we can sympathize with the plight of a three-legged Buffalo!

As all these microcosms of variety collecting illustrate, there is no limit to the breadth and

The three-legged Buffalo nickel is missing the right foreleg – we can sympathize with the beast! Heavy-handed grinding (or lapping) was the cause, as the dies had previously clashed together without a coin in-between and needed repair.

challenge of the field. The hunt for new varieties can continue indefinitely. Consequently, the goal of completion becomes more elusive and is more dependent on how the collector defines the limits of the set. Once you get out on the die variety frontier, it becomes clear that the collection will never be completed – tell *that* to your spouse!

The typical jumping off point for series collectors who are intrigued by all this is to add one or more of the major *Red Book* listed varieties to the set. We have seen that this stimulates our curiosity by injecting manageable amounts of novelty and complexity into our collecting. Certainly, the bold 1955 doubled-die cent would represent a good start for the Lincoln cent collector – it is the consummate example of this type of variety. Similarly, re-punched and over-mintmarks could be added, as the *Red Book* describes several to choose from; for example, the 1944-D over S cent can be easily appreciated. How about the 1922 plain cent? Once the popular varieties are acquired, the collector is left to ponder the uncharted territory of lesser-known die varieties listed in the "cherry-picking" and specialist guides.

We can joke about how more and more is learned about less and less, and how the wide world of numismatics is pursued through the narrow lens of the magnifying glass. Yet, the die variety enthusiast is likely to be having great fun delving into the small palate enclosed within the rims. Like a spiraling whirlpool found in a fairytale, it sucks you in, and you discover a whole universe filled with others who deeply share your passion. The quest for die varieties moves the date and mint collector well beyond the regimen of the completist and into the realm of the scholar. And frankly, we are indebted.

For best results in hunting die varieties a metallurgical microscope with a micrometer stage is needed ... this instrument measures to a hundred thousandth of an inch, which should be adequate for all but the most die-hard of variety collectors. With this instrument an entire new world of exploration is opened, and the number of varieties waiting to be discovered becomes infinite.

The Lincoln Memorial shows twelve columns in need of examination under the microscope. These columns vary in thickness from .0275 to .0306 of an inch based on sample number of measurements made with this microscope.

The possible number of combinations of three thicknesses of the twelve columns is one million, five hundred ninety-four thousand, three hundred and twenty-three (1,594,323), which should provide a challenging start to the serious die variety enthusiast.

— *Excerpts from: Michael M. Dolnick,* The Numismatist *(Vol. 74),* January 1961

"We want to build collections of our own design. We are striving to shape, and thereby understand, the world we live in."

A Need
for Order

I fondly remember those Saturday mornings when I pulled out my blue
Lincoln folder – the old one that started with 1909 – to take stock. I began the
ritual by punching them all out on the kitchen table. I retrieved the rusty tin of
Brasso from under the sink. A fresh white facecloth was secreted away from the
bathroom on which I would cover the spout and flip it upside-down to produce a
circular blot of thick purplish paste. With a vigorous thumb, the cleanings began.
I mashed each cent into the cloth and rubbed hard, until under tap water, the
coin sparkled with a golden sheen.

Once cleaned and dried, I arranged them in rows by date. This was my
favorite part of the ritual – arranging and rearranging. I had one from every
year except 1915, 1922, and 1931. Very few were from San Francisco. But I had
a 1910-S in full good condition! This one received special attention – I kept it
glossy! I took great pride in my collection. I had found each one. These were my
cents, and I was their master! I could organize them anyway I wanted to: by date,

by mint. After each one had been inspected, I lined them up and punched them in taking note of the dull thump that signaled a snug fit in the folder.

A series of coins, painstakingly assembled, is a matter of pride. Countless bank rolls were searched and difficult trades were negotiated along the way. This was an epic quest for a 9-year-old! Each find told the story of a successful hunt. A collecting script had been written, one cent at a time.

As we all can agree, a collection of Lincoln cents, laid out in a folder, provides a pleasing visual display. It has rhythm: identical faces aligned in rows like a drum-beat, with accents interspersed where "special" coins shine brighter or boast of rarity. Vacant holes produce sharp cadences, marking still missing coins. These vacancies represented my hopes and dreams – rewards yet to come. My future was clear.

Coin boards, first introduced in the late 1930s, provided a template for organizing a small part of an otherwise chaotic world. The empty holes represented a challenge that introduced novelty into pocket change. Complexity increased as the game unfolded; the remaining coins were harder and harder to find. Casual cent board collectors grew frustrated and simply gave up. They lost interest. But those with a burning desire to have them

Polishing up the 1910-S. Coin care rituals are an essential part of collecting. The experienced collector takes pride in adopting high curatorial standards to protect their coins from harmful elements – like Brasso!

all soldiered on. They were determined to complete the set, to master the game.

The feeling of control is an important part of the collecting experience. In no small way, collectors control their destiny by assembling a set of coins. It is with great pride that the Lincoln cent collector stands back and surveys the completed folder and exclaims, "I made this!" Non-collectors can be perplexed by this attitude: "Why not go to a museum if you want to see them?" When social researchers ask collectors this very question, they always get the same answers. The responses get right to the point: "Because it is not yours," and "You cannot touch them." Having control is everything. You have not mastered the game if you are not in control.

Autonomy is a powerful motivator for collecting. Collectors exercise supreme control over their coins. Jean Baudrillard, author of *The System of Objects*, added that the collector controls the objects thereby "imposing order on a small part of the world." He goes on to note that "surrounded by the objects he possesses, the collector is pre-eminently the sultan of a secret seraglio." These statements underscore a theme that most students of collecting embrace: *collecting provides a sense of mastery over a chaotic world.* Susan Steward, in her book *On Longing*, has taken the symbolism a step further in suggesting that the fascination with miniatures – from dollhouses to toy soldiers to matchbox cars – is rooted in childhood play geared toward ruling a "homemade universe."

Of course, seasoned coin collectors refrain from the kitchen table play of 9-year olds. The urge to touch is still present, but this desire is funneled into a set of codified rules of engagement. In short, coins must be treated in a certain way. Consequently, the collector gains mastery by becoming an expert coin handler. The underlying dynamic is the same, however. The desire for control is played out in the development of specialized numismatic skills.

Becoming an expert at condition grading is a prime example of how collectors gain a sense of mastery. These newfound skills not only help us build better collections, but also they set us apart from others. The process is a natural one that most can identify with. After searching through pocket change and dealer inventories, the Lincoln cent collector will be faced with decisions about what to do when confronted with duplicates of higher quality. Duplicates initiate upgrading. And upgrading leads to the development of a new set of numismatic skills. A keen eye for subtle variations in strike, luster, and wear is honed. As we have seen, determining the grade of a Lincoln cent, or any coin, is an advanced skill – but one that rewards us with better collections *and* a greater sense of mastery.

It is no wonder that condition grading is the hottest topic in numismatics. More than money is on the line. To become a master collector, you must be able to grade coins. Scott Travers devotes nearly half of his popular, and aptly named book, *The Coin Collector's Survival Manual* to grading issues. His introduction to the topic is enough to intimidate even the seasoned collector.

> *Grading. It sounds like a simple word and a description of a simple process. The word itself may be simple, but the process it describes in the field of coins couldn't be more complex. The variables related to grading are endless. The debate among knowledgeable numismatists about what affects grade or why coins are graded remains unsettled. The country's foremost numismatists are undecided as to what grading really is.*

Clearly, learning how to become a master collector is not easy. Indeed, the cent collector cannot control his destiny without competent grading skills. Some collectors suffer through condition grading seminars, as it is deemed necessary to learn (but not that enjoyable to sit through). Knowledge of grading principles leads to well-informed purchases, and we all agree that acquiring a marvelous coin is the goal. Hence, learning to grade is a means to an end. Once our grading skills are developed, and it becomes second nature, the grading process becomes enjoyable. It is deeply rewarding in the same way that pouring over your Lincoln cents on the kitchen table used to be.

Of course, condition grading and all the other rules for collecting become internalized over time. They become your rules. When I finally stopped scrubbing my Lincoln cents, I still had the urge to rub my finger across them to feel the slick copper. But I learned to resist this urge. It violated the rules of numismatic correctness. Yet, the feel of cool copper is still alluring, even to this day. At first, I had to remind myself of the potential harm that can come from oily fingers and added friction. Later, I just imposed the rule without thinking about it; I had internalized the rule. It was my rule!

As this discussion reveals, numismatics is a rule-governed activity. We cherish this because these rules reflect our dedication and mastery. Those who do not collect think we are obsessed with order and procedure. They think we are preoccupied with the minutest of details. But they miss the point. We want control. We want to build collections of our own design. We are striving to shape and thereby understand the world we live in. Perhaps the best analogy is that we are forming our own little museum. We are the owners, but also the curators. As curators we have to follow strict rules.

We also have to decide what exhibit to create next. An arrangement of coins on the dining room table tells a unique story of our choosing. The storyline can reflect our interpretation of history. Or, the storyline can be about our own quest to acquire one of each. What is included or excluded is wholly up to us. In each case, the narrative is different and multifaceted. Lincoln cents spread out on the table tell a story of devotion to numismatics and the power of ownership; they also tell the story of a revered president and a nation of penny board collectors during the Great Depression.

Maybe this is the greatest of all powers: the ability to tell stories. To organize the world as it happened. What is collecting but a meaningful sequence of events that produces a narrative of our hopes and dreams? As Mieke Bal observed in his essay *Telling Objects: A Narrative Perspective on Collecting:* "Collecting is an essential human feature that originates in the need to tell stories, but for which there are neither words nor other conventional narrative modes. Hence, collecting is a story, and everyone needs to tell it."

If there is an allusion to playing God here,
perhaps it is apt. The collector as the creator of the
collection assumes the role of possessor, controller,
and sometimes saviour of the objects collected.

— *Russell Belk,* Collecting in a Consumer Society. 1995

"As it becomes apparent that we are not alone, we begin to search for our niche. I wanted to know about the large cent collectors. Did they all wear plaid shirts?"

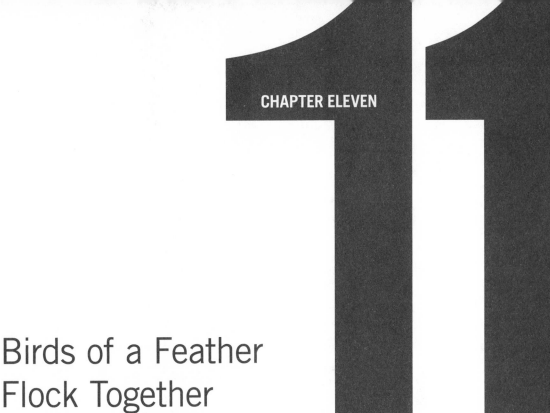

CHAPTER ELEVEN

Birds of a Feather Flock Together

Coffeehouse talk in my neighborhood is usually about rain and local misadventures, but rarely is it about coins. Sharing my Internet auction triumphs is a sure conversation stopper. Instead, I am often faced with explaining myself to incredulous non-collectors. The sensibility of any explanation, beyond the faint notion that coins might represent good investments, is questioned. Appeals to historic and artistic merit are often met with vacant stares and forced smiles. And so I have learned to mute my expressions of numismatic passion. Coin talk is kept brief. I find it prudent to skip the gory details – like having just spent several hundred dollars on a few cents of old money!

Collecting can be a lonesome pastime. It is like playing solitaire. My mind may be swirling with tidbits of history, but I am alone with my thoughts. Internet auction sites consume my Saturday mornings at the expense of more social activities. It is an odd feeling to be so interested in something that others find painfully boring! On occasion, I am stifled by the lack of interest: I want to shout

out how I scored a remarkable cent at the risk of being labeled a pubic nuisance!

It is true that many collectors are quietly amused. We might mistakenly think that collectors are introverted types who prefer objects to people. This would be wrong. Pick any collector, and feigning all the sincerity you can muster, ask them to tell you about their stuff. You will be surprised at what you get. The following sketch provided by Rigby and Rigby in *Lock, Stock, and Barrel: The Story of Collecting* captures this inner light:

> *[A] collector of your acquaintance may seem the most silent of men,
> a tongue-tied individual with no apparent interests, difficult to know
> or to befriend, but try mentioning something, anything, remotely
> connected with his collecting field and you will see lamps in his eyes
> brighten. His tongue will be unloosened as though by magic, and he
> will take you into his heart for life.*

With such passions within us, it is inevitable that we become restless and reach out. Numismatic magazines offer a quick fix. Within these pages, the collector realizes that thousands of kindred spirits are out there. We discover that there are others who are as obsessed as we are. I find this deeply comforting. I want reassurance. Here begins a socialization process that often leads to coin show attendance, local coin club participation, and membership in national organizations.

For many collectors, life-long friendships are forged in the context of these events. This is true throughout the collecting subculture: antique cars, tin toys, primitive furniture, and coins – all bring people together. It should not be surprising that many collectors report that these friendships represent the most important part of numismatics. In fact, the need for "belongingness" is so universal that most psychologists view it as a primary human motivation that underlies how people view themselves.

When we adopt the identity of a collector, we expand our sense of self. It is a new role we get to play – an opportunity to recast who we are. I have defined myself as a husband, psychologist, and runner. To that, I add coin collector. I am more complex because I collect. I take special pride in having adopted this role; for example, I can recall esoteric bits of numismatic history like a contestant on *Jeop-*

ardy. And I can do it all day long. *How many varieties of Chain cents are there? Five.*

Early on, I fancied myself as a Renaissance man even though I was not exactly sure what that was. Such men know about coins. Then I met a tin toy collector who boasted that he was a Renaissance man too! Maybe he was, but he did not collect coins. I finally gave up on the notion when a matchbook collector told me the same thing. Are we all Renaissance men? I was curious about who these other folks were – and what made them tick. Yet, I desperately wanted to interact with my own collecting brethren. To know about coin collectors is to know about me.

We often start the socialization process by learning the rules of the game, everything from how to handle coins to coin shop etiquette. In addition, the standards of what the average coin collector should know are gleaned from guidebooks and periodicals. Finally we identify with core values regarding the appreciation of art and the preservation, and reverence for, history. This socialization process nurtures an intense curiosity about the mysterious ways of coin collectors. Maybe I was becoming a Renaissance man after all.

The opportunities for developing a sense of belongingness are numerous in our Internet era. Free to join and available 24-hours a day, numismatic forums provide quick and easy access to a large community. A recent survey of several popular forums found 12,000+ threads with hundreds of active discussions at any given time. Over 16,000 collectors claimed membership. The most popular threads – those with the most replies – were on social topics that addressed personal interests, ethical dilemmas, and collecting goals.

As it becomes apparent that we are not alone, we begin to search for our niche. I wanted to know about the large cent collectors. Did they all wear plaid shirts? This seemed like essential information at the time. Knowing them promised to define my identity in ways that I had not thought of. Of course, we all wonder why we collect and others do not. But what I really wanted to know was what makes someone chase after battered large cents?

Simply being a member of the coin collecting fraternity is one thing, but joining a specialist group within numismatics is the *crème de la crème* of belongingness. For example, the collector of early copper cents and half cents can join the *Early American Copper Society*; this club offers a quarterly journal entitled, *Penny-Wise,* that provides information on the history, grading, and collecting of these coins. In addition, the members get together in the spring to share news, swap coins, and tell stories. Subgroups flourish within the organization too, such as the *Boys of 94* who are dedicated to collecting the 56+ varieties of Liberty Cap cents dated 1794. There is something for everyone if you look hard enough. Specialty groups exist for almost any niche you can think of: from the *Full-step Jefferson Nickel Club* to the *Silver Dollar Roundtable*. These groups increase homogeneity in nearly all aspects of coin collecting – hunting, grading, and preservation, as well as historical focus – thereby tightening the feelings of kinship.

In a curious process called *self-stereotyping*, collectors who identify with a particular group begin to see themselves as similar to its members. Consequently, they view themselves as having similar values and perspectives. The surprising thing is, this occurs despite the absence of actual interpersonal interactions; rather we become kindred spirits in an abstract way, gleaned from club newsletters plus any notions that we had before. In this way, feelings of camaraderie are accelerated.

After a few years of reading newsletters, I attended the annual meeting of the *Early American Coppers Society*. What I found was a striking mix of personalities. Here was a bunch of men (mostly) from all walks of life bonded by a love of copper coins. And no, they did not wear plaid shirts. Tales of collecting triumphs and missed opportunities filled the room. It was as if the whole world revolved around collecting old copper coins!

For those who join, membership in a specialized group provides the collector with *highly relevant* opportunities for social comparison. It would be hard to find this opportunity anywhere else. For example, possession of specific knowledge confers status: this is particularly true in tight-knit groups where skills, such as die-variety attribution, are appreciated. Knowing how to accurately recognize the configuration of leaves in the wreath of a 1796 cent requires expertise that is highly valued. Where else could you get a pat on the back for knowing such stuff?

In addition, collecting clubs herald each member's collection as a status symbol. Even a meager collection – like mine – is likely to be revered among the faithful few who share the same interests. Pride in ownership is sweeter when shared with others. As such, specialty groups provide members with a ready vehicle for gaining status among one's peers. Indeed, I have found that everyone wants to see my battered chain cent!

In a related vein, one advantage of joining a collecting fraternity is that members are open and accepting to whomever wants to learn the ways of the specialist. Collecting clubs are democratic. Russell Belk has characterized collecting as a leveler of social class in his book *Collecting in a Consumer Society*:

> *Even though the wealthiest collectors in any area tend to have an advantage in being able to afford the most admired and status-imparting objects, other collectors' knowledge, time, persistence, and luck can compensate to some degree. Along with choosing an affordable and narrow collecting area and specialty with this area, these factors make it possible for a large number of people from all but the lowest social classes to find opportunities for success in collecting.*

In this way, cherry picking strategies offer equal opportunity to all collectors willing to learn and apply these skills. Much of the folklore shared in coin collecting groups involves these tales of conquest!

In contrast to social bonding within the group, membership also provides a

context for defining how one is different from others. Distinctiveness is perhaps the most important aspect of the self. We all want to stand out in some way. Hence, my youthful aspirations to be regarded as a Renaissance man!

At this point, we come full circle, as we are reminded of the solitary collector who is barraged with questions about why they are passionate about coins. The potential for an existential crisis is real. Why am I so enthralled with large cents? How could I spend so much money on them? I ask these questions from time to time. It should not be surprising that many collectors have struggled to come up with satisfying answers. In this regard, psychologists have proposed that one of the chief functions of group membership involves the reduction of uncertainty about whom we have chosen to be.

Uncertainty is uncomfortable. And uncertainty about collecting is even more uncomfortable – particularly when you have a box of coins under your bed. Having just spent several thousands of dollars on a marvelous coin has the potential of plunging the collector into a cycle of self-doubt and recrimination. This discomfort is familiar terrain wherein emotions and reason often clash. And the knife of uncertainty is given an added twist when well-intentioned non-collectors ask the intrusive question: *why coins?*

Group membership serves to reduce this discomfort. We know that our collecting friends understand. One of the first things I find myself doing after spending big money on a coin is to show it to collecting friends: they know what it is all about, and at some deeper level, I feel better. Our desire for belongingness is often guided by needs for validation. This need is best met when you feel connected to a tight, highly relevant, collecting fraternity such as a specialist group.

On balance, coin collectors flock together as numismatics provides a rich social identity. Some collectors are outgoing by nature and find the bourse ripe with camaraderie, whereas others – quiet and reserved about their hobby – still feel connected to the larger fraternity via the media. Either way, the social aspects of coin collecting are essential in providing deep reassurance that we are not alone and that the whole enterprise is alive and meaningful.

My greatest numismatic interest is not so much

in coins as in travel and meeting with fellow

collectors around the country. … Famous authors,

sculptors, and Mint officials have all been part

of the wonderful group of people that I have had

the privilege of meeting during my coin collecting

activities. … Along with my enjoyment of coins

is the satisfaction I have found in helping young

numismatists to become involved and to learn

about the wonderful world of coins in a way that

will hopefully last a lifetime.

— Florence Schook, Past President of the American Numismatic Association, quote
in Q. David Bowers, The Numismatist's Downtown Companion, 1994

"What a liberating

way to collect coins.

You never know

exactly where it is

going to lead you."

Getting Started: Collecting by Design Type

CHAPTER TWELVE

I have a few State quarters. Well, actually I have all of them plus the funky fold-out map to put them in. It is not my specialty; in fact, I cannot tell you why Arkansas has a diamond on it, or what kind of dinosaur is flying over Mount Rushmore. But I have to save one of each; I cannot resist the urge. I reflexively examine the quarters I am about to spend just to see which ones I am letting go. Sometimes I hold the Connecticut ones back because I like the big tree. All those states, territories, and parks – a true collector is drawn to this kind of diversity like a moth to the light.

Pocket change demanded a second glance in 1999. Delaware's Paul Revere design led the charge exclaiming, "The states are coming; the states are coming." Within months, ordinary coins were making a statement. It was loud enough to pique the curiosity of a rushed and distracted public. New designs were appearing as quickly as the weather was changing: Pennsylvania, New Jersey, Georgia, and Connecticut. This created anticipation and guessing. At the height of the

The State quarter program introduced collecting by design type to millions of American collectors.

program, the United States Mint estimated that 139 million Americans were collecting the new State quarters.

Television and magazine promotions encouraged many upstart collectors to purchase "complete" 50-state sets. But few took the initiative to explore the quarters that came before – after all, they all looked the same. They were still just pocket change. Nonetheless, a seed was planted and the search for more "types" of coins was under way, prompted by the question: What was the Mint going to do next? For our youngest generation of coin collectors, collecting by design type had become synonymous with numismatics.

The Mint has not disappointed those who wanted to add to their type collections. The Westward Journey nickels of 2004 and 2005, plus the Monticello design of 2006 spiced-up the once stolid Jefferson nickels series, and Abraham Lincoln's bicentennial was celebrated

The evolution of design types within a denomination allows the collector to assemble a uniform set that explores how Ms. Liberty changed over time and circumstance.

in 2009 with four new reverse designs on the cent – plus a new shield reverse for 2010. The National Park quarter series debuted in 2010 and is scheduled to last a decade. All of this is in addition to the roll call of past Presidents (four per year) coupled with the annual celebration of Native American heritage on our one-dollar coins. There have been so many new designs that some collectors are feeling overwhelmed by their efforts to keep up with them all.

For seasoned collectors, the notion of type collecting has been around for a long time but has remained on the periphery. In fact, a type set comprised of 20th century coins used to be considered a layman's exercise: it made a nice gift or wall display. Nowadays, the set has exploded in size and diversity, offering quite a challenge just to identify them all. Add in a few subtypes from the variety collecting tradition and the prospect of type collecting can become a viable numismatic specialty all its own. In addition, collecting one of each design type offers several distinct advantages over series collecting.

For starters, devotion to a single series have become more frustrating for some, as nicer key coins have become more difficult to find. Consequently, set completion goals have become harder to accomplish. For example, if you extended your State quarter collection back to the start of the Washington quarter series, you might be shocked to find that the values of Mint State 1932 quarters from Denver and San Francisco have more than doubled in the past five years – these are the two low-mintage keys of the series.

With such high demand pushing up coin prices for quality coins, the once reasonable prospect of completing a complete run of quarters from the Barber series to date is daunting. A series collector could spend the better part of a lifetime assembling a high to medium grade set of Standing Liberty and Barber quarters. Of course, there is nothing wrong with that! However, many collectors do not have the budget, or the fortitude, to go the distance. Predictably, collecting trends have gone the other way toward an in-depth focus on a single series, or even a shortened set.

Type collecting circumvents some of these difficulties by offering up a broader collecting plan that allows the collector to pursue more reasonable goals. In this regard, a type set of 20th century does not require the key coins so that the collector's best efforts can be directed toward selecting coins that are of a higher grade and more satisfying to own. For example, an early 1930s Washington quarter can be purchased in MS-63 for under $50 in lieu of an expensive branch mint key that is less attractive in a lesser grade. And just think how nice it would be to have a choice Mint State Barber quarter to start off with!

Another advantage of type collecting is that collectors can explore more series of coins than would otherwise be possible. Many early series have beautiful designs that some collectors never get to experience owning due to a strict allegiance to set completion goals in another series. One of my favorites is Liberty Seated quarters minted from 1838 to 1891. To focus on completing the series itself would be extremely difficult, as the Carson City (CC) coins alone would bust budgets and end marriages. But it would be satisfying to have a few nice ones – a type set would allow you to do this.

In a similar vein, type collecting allows collectors to own gold. With high prices tied to a bullion market that has spiked to nearly $1,500 per ounce, few collectors can consider putting together a series of gold coins. In addition, there are many great rarities in the series; in fact, most coins from North Carolina or Georgia are rare and expensive. Yet, a type set of Liberty and Indian coins is reasonably priced with most of the larger denominations selling for a small premium over bullion values. Why deny yourself a gold coin if you have always

A type set allows collectors to explore many interesting colonial coins that are often overlooked. This is unfortunate, as these historic cents and half-cents are relatively inexpensive and are full of early American imagery.

wanted one? And what better way is there for the collector-investor to build a meaningful collection?

One of the more esoteric areas of numismatics that is gaining popularity and lends itself to type collecting is the field of colonial numismatics. A wide variety of coins circulated in North American during the colonial era and the early years of the Republic prior to the founding of the federal mint in 1792. These coins – primarily cents and half-cents – are typically collected by types and die varieties. Nearly all guides to United States coins include a section detailing these issues. I think it sad that many series collectors fail to take advantage of owning such historically important coins despite affordable prices for many of them in nice circulated grades. Have you considered owning a Fugio copper of 1787? This was the first coin authorized by the federal government!

On balance, perhaps the most appealing aspect of type collecting is that this approach allows the most flexibility to have it your way. Whereas series collectors hold fast to the proverbial confines of the coin folder, type collectors are actively defining and shaping the direction of the collection as they go. Type collectors are invigorated with the novelty of new designs and are less likely to get bored or bogged down with expensive key coins that cannot be acquired in pleasing grades.

The most straightforward starting point for the type collector is to define a set by its era, denomination, or metallic composition. I remember when 20th century sets were popular in the 1970s; a number of dealers marketed coin folders for these sets. This is a great starter set, as all the coins can be acquired in Mint State condition with moderate effort and budget. From circulation, a type set collector today can start with post-1965 coinage and work forward to include new issues as they are produced – once you consider all the state and national park quarters, plus the circulating commemorative coins, this would produce quite a large collection at face value.

Although type sets have relatively clear boundaries, the collector would need to discriminate between types and subtypes in order to decide what coins merit inclusion. The nomenclature that differentiates between certain die varieties and subtypes is not always clear. Nonetheless, most experts define a subtype as a characteristic – a design or composition change – that was intended for use. Yet, some subtypes are subtle and are considered to be more akin to die varieties. For me, I think this is where the fun begins: namely, deciding which coin you want to pursue next and why.

Lincoln cents provide a several prime examples of these decision points. Certainly an example of the 1943 steel cents would be included; but what about the 1944-1945 shell casing cents or the zinc core verses no zinc core cents of 1982? Here you must decide how important metallic content will be in your collection. Certainly the different reverse designs – the wheat ear (1909-1958) versus the Lincoln Memorial (1959-2008) – would be included, but what about more subtle improvements on the obverse that includes small and large dates in 1960 and a modified hub in 1969? Here again, you must ask yourself, what do I see as important?

Ultimately, it is up to you to decide which subtypes to include. This is where the type collector can exercise their numismatic acumen and creativity to bring the significance of particular subtypes or varieties into focus. In this way, the collector is developing a storyline that ties together historical tidbits to produce intrigue, just as a novelist would do. As the collector develops more knowledge,

Thematic collecting is shaped by one's imagination; in this case, cash crops make for bountiful wreaths. Can you find the wheat, corn, and cotton?

more subtypes or varieties can be added; for example, the Lincoln cents of late 1909 to 1917 are without any designer's initials whereas cents from 1918 onward have a VDB placed under the shoulder of Lincoln's bust; in addition, the obverse hub that produced the working dies for the cent (and Buffalo nickel) were reworked in 1916 to produce a seldom appreciated subtype – you decide: should these subtypes be included?

Another way to add intrigue to a type set is to include both first and last year coins; this feature concretely defines the era when the coins were produced. One specimen from each mint extends the set even further. Alternatively, the well-heeled collector might decide to form a type set that contains some of the key coins of the series: how about a 1909-S VDB for a Lincoln cent type set? I sure would like to have one! Again, herein lies the allure of the type collecting: you can have it your way.

Perhaps the most unrestrained approach to type collecting is to pursue a theme, like collecting eagles or wreaths. The bald eagle appears on all early silver coins as well as on contemporary quarters, halves, and dollars. The images vary widely, from the strong, stoic eagle perched on a rock found on the 1921 Peace dollar to the scrawny, annoyed eagle, twisting it head to look straight at you on the 1794 Flowing Hair dollar. Our symbols come in many postures and attitudes. An impressive array of images could be collected that tells something about art, politics, and our national character.

In a similar fashion, the agricultural output of the North American continent could be enjoyed in the rich variety of wreaths found on half-cents through dimes. Quite a diversity is evidenced just on small cents: the Flying Eagle cents depict a wreath of corn, wheat, cotton, and tobacco, whereas the 1859 Indian cents show a laurel wreath that was replaced with an oak wreath in the following year – of course, two elegant wheat stalks came later when the Lincoln cent was introduced in 1909. Our earliest cents show a simple two-branch olive wreath wherein each leaf was punched in separately to produce hand-woven festoons as varied as those found at a farmer's market.

Thematic collections come closest to the notion of aesthetic collecting where passion and curiosity drives the collecting process. Eagles and wreaths certainly appeal to our sense of artistry; but as the above observations suggest, much can be learned from paying attention to the posture of the great birds and the contents of the wreaths. Consequently, the thematic collector can approach their topic as rigorously as desired, for iconography is an often over-looked aspect of numismatics.

Breaking from the mold of series collecting provides a way for collectors to uniquely define themselves. I have collected both ways: I have sets of buffalo nickels and large cents, but I also have a few colonial types, not to mention those wonderful pieces of eight! What a liberating way to collect coins. You never know exactly where it is going to lead you. Type collectors still set goals for themselves, but you are making them up as you discover new opportunities. If you want something totally different every time you go to the coin bourse, then this is for you: "Hmm, today I think I'll look at the Fugio coppers."

"For collectors, a personal attachment to, or reverence for, special coins takes precedence over price."

Addictive Numismaticitis

Coin collectors are the first to admit that their behavior is eccentric. Some even claim to have a numismatic addiction. This is not an uncommon notion among collectors who try to make sense of their incessant quest for the next coin. The demand to justify "collecting" becomes ever more acute when confronted by inquiring non-collectors. Friends, family, and spouses are mystified by the insatiable desire.

The social awkwardness of the collecting life is not new. In the October 1876 issue of the *American Journal of Numismatics* one writer remarked, "It is not surprising that many persons are disposed to regard the mania for 'collecting,' as it is termed, as puerile and ridiculous, when it is directed to articles of no intrinsic interest or importance." Like many collectors, he went on to defend coin collecting for its historical merits.

Half a century later, another commentator wrote in *The Numismatist* that, in response to coin talk, "some will listen and look at you with a blank stare; others will smile tolerantly as though to say 'Crazy, but harmless.'" Before long, the collector learns to manage these responses. But, sometimes it is just easier to shout, "I'm addicted!" and be done with it. That usually halts all inquiries.

An addiction to coins has sparked prose. In 1946, George Pipes offered this verse to readers of *The Numismatist*:

> *What is the group that is gathering here?*
> *They call them Numismatists, they seem kinda queer.*
> *Why do they come here? Old coins they collect.*
> *And hope to get more of them, hope and expect;*
> *And they show to each other the coins they have gotten*
> *So the rest will feel envious, covetous, rotten.*
> *I make this indictment without an apology,*
> *For that is our nature, that is psychology.*

The verse is humorous. Coin collectors are "kinda queer," but there is also edginess in the poetry: coin collectors are "envious, covetous, rotten." This juxtaposition of positive and negative permeates the reflections and commentary about the supposition that collecting is driven by addiction.

In 1981 *The Numismatist* author William Nawrocki described the term "Numismaticitis" as a "non-fatal social disease" that is highly contagious and without cure. Reckless irrationality was listed as a prominent symptom: "If the numismatist's home were engulfed in flames, the stout-hearted collector would risk life and limb to bail out his specimens … after retrieving these precious treasures, he might think about his wife and children." Clearly, the condition can be dangerous to self and others!

Another collector likened the behaviors of coin collectors to "the craziness of moths." The idea of addiction and disease is common and not limited to numismatics. In a survey of 13,000 American collectors conducted several decades ago, more than

70 percent admitted they were addicted to their hobby. Social scientists have suggested that appeals to a "disease model" of collecting are best understood as a way to avoid embarrassment while disclaiming responsibility for collecting behaviors that others find irrational. Yet, such claims expose an undercurrent of concern and curiosity among collectors themselves, particularly as they spend countless hours and oodles of cash pursuing numismatic treasures.

In this era of third-party grading and rare coin investment consultants, it appears that financial return is the reigning model of numismatic correctness. This preserves the illusion that collectors are making rational choices. It is hard to argue otherwise when collectors arm themselves with "Red Books," "Blue Books" and "Grey Sheets" – all part of a methodical strategy to select high-quality, rare and underappreciated coins, with an eye toward future appreciation.

This approach has become the norm in the marketplace, given the scores of limited edition collectibles produced and hawked as great investments. Even the United States Mint has jumped into the fray, offering a dizzying variety of commemoratives, bullion coins, and proofs. Nonetheless, many coin collectors remain addled in confronting their numismatic passions that transcend market considerations.

Russell Belk, writing in the *Journal of Social Behavior and Personality*, has argued that the notion of the rational collector is a myth. He has presented six tests to determine if an object – in this case, a coin – is of "a more numinous character."

Test #1: Refusal to sell the coin at full market value. Items of "sentimental" value provide ready examples. Ask any collector with a tattered Whitman folder of Lincoln cents (nearly completed while in grade school, but of course missing the 1909-S VDB, 1914-D and 1922 "No D") if he would sell the contents at full retail price. He will probably say "no," as nostalgia weighs heavily. And how about that rare Liberty Cap large cent (a Sheldon-48 "starred reverse") cherrypicked from a dealer's junk box? That one was a triumph of die-variety attribution, a storied coin in the annals of numismatics! No, some coins are simply not for sale. For collectors, a personal attachment to, or reverence for, special

Collectors act irrationally much of the time. They cannot resist coins, putting themselves at risk for sore fingers time and again.

coins takes precedence over price. This is an irrational stance in the numismatic marketplace.

Test #2: Willingness to purchase a coin at any cost, or at least with little regard for market price. Many collectors will pay at bit more for a key coin with good eye appeal, but market analysts are surprised when common date, modern coins in "registry set grades" of Mint State (MS)-67, -68, -69 sell for thousands. Auction competition is fierce, and record sales are commonplace. In January 2001, a 1953 Franklin half dollar with full bell lines, graded MS-66 by Professional Coin Grading Service (PCGS), sold for $69,000, prompting pundits to ponder, "Is this tulip bulb mania?" Many of these sales constitute irrational behavior, but some collectors argue that such coins are unique examples of ultimate minted beauty and are required for top-rank collections.

Test #3: Belief that no two coins are created equal. In a rational market, one MS-64 Morgan dollar is the same as any other MS-64 Morgan dollar. However, many collectors insist that each coin is unique with regard to strike, luster, wear, and eye appeal; consequently, one coin cannot be substituted for another. Numismatists readily accept this reality for all collectible coins, but in rational, economic terms, this is untenable. In contrast, non-collectible coins *are* the same: one worn and scratched 1965 quarter is as good as the next; in practice, coins that are considered "just change" are, in a sense, dateless – we do not care if it is dated 1965 or 1966.

Test #4: Unwillingness to spend certain coins that freely circulate. This is a "threshold" test, as it draws the line between coins that are spent and those that are kept. Deciding whether to set aside a Lincoln cent with the Wheat Ear reverse illustrates this test – the cent's utility is no longer considered once set aside (of course, the utility of the cent is already in question due to its low purchasing power). Sometimes this threshold changes: young collectors who decide to "punch out" a few wheaties to satisfy their craving for something sweet. The same can be said regarding the decision to save a Virginia State quarter thereby ignoring its utility as money. This is irrational.

Test #5: Emotional reactions to a coin or collection. Simply put, the passion that a numismatist experiences when he interacts with coins is unexpected in a heavily commoditized coin market where appraised value and investment potential are paramount. From the euphoria of winning a desired coin at auction to the soothing sense of well-being that a collector often feels when he views his coins, these wide-ranging emotions underscore how significant coins have become in his life. There is no shortage of love and conquest stories in the collecting world, as noted in the book *Lock, Stock and Barrel: The Story of Collecting* (1944): "The emotions of such a collector ... are the emotions of a Don Juan engaged in forming a harem, and each item added to the collection-harem is a symbol of a new conquest seen through a rosy veil of illusion."

Test #6: Personification of coins. A simple gendering of Liberty will suffice ("She is beautiful with ribbons in her hair.") Some collectors name one or more of their coins, as in the case of a large cent collector, writing in the January 2003 edition of *Penny-Wise*, who named all his coppers "Edna" and described his passion for his "mistress." As Russell Belk observed, when we name our possessions and treat them like human beings, "they become not things, but people, infused with life and personality."

Given the inescapable irrationality of coin collecting, as illustrated by these six tests described above, it is not surprising that many collectors have confessed their addiction to coins. One does not need a degree in psychoanalysis to see the defensive motive here. Responsibility for irrational choices is defused, and collectors can be excused for paying too much or refusing to sell at a profit. After all, addictions are not completely under our control.

Yet, in a curious twist, self-diagnosis has become fashionable. To indulge in the "collecting bug" or "auction fever" is commonplace. And what should we make of the Bust Half Nut Club, in which membership is offered only to those "nuts" with powerful loupes and at least 100 different die varieties of half dollars minted between 1807 and 1836? In this context, having a "bug" or being a "nut" is an endearment, similar to the 14th-century use of the word "addict" as one who is devoted. Nonetheless, contemporary references to "addiction" almost exclusively point to a disease process by which one becomes dependent on a particular substance, an object, or a behavior.

Nicotine, alcohol, amphetamines, and narcotics are the substances most

The distorted world of the collector addicted to copper coins.

often associated with addictions these days. They produce pleasurable feelings by stimulating brain circuitry associated with chemicals such as dopamine and glutamate. This system rewards behaviors that lead to friendships and feelings of competence and status. As such, when we make good decisions in life, we are rewarded with a boost of pleasure-producing biochemistry. This is one of the reasons love and friendships feel so good.

The problem with cigarettes, beer, weight-loss pills, and painkillers is that these substances short-circuit the reward system, providing immediate pleasure at levels far exceeding those produced by living well and making good decisions. Furthermore, the brain becomes sensitized to drug cues, and intense cravings develop. Consequently, substance abusers devote less time to normal routines of work, family, and leisure.

Can the repeated acquisition of highly coveted coins produce the same result in collectors? Does an exaggerated dopamine rush lead to intense cravings? Can coins act as biochemical stimulants powerful enough to corrupt our normal incentive system? For numismatic addiction to be a valid medical condition, one would expect to see a pattern of uncontrolled, repetitive searching for coins that replaces, or crowds out, social and vocational activities. In addition, one would see this potentially destructive pattern continue despite failed attempts to stop collecting.

Numismatic vignettes that reflect behaviors similar to addictive cravings are not hard to find. For example, in his book *The History of United States Coinage as Illustrated by the Garrett Collection*, Q. David Bowers quotes the illustrious Lyman Low, known for his research on hard times tokens, who described his interest in coins in the 1870s: "My ardor was thoroughly aroused, and the interest I took was intense. I dreamed and talked of coins incessantly." Taken at face value, this admission certainly suggests a crowding-out of other activities. We can only guess how others may have reacted to his "incessant" coin talk!

But is this addiction or love? Often extreme displays of irrationality in the pursuit of coins are touted as diagnostic. Observations of "wild" bidding and busted budgets beg the question. Yet stories of coin collectors needing ever-larger coin fixes fail to be convincing. There is simply no evidence to suggest that hunting for coins corrupts body biochemistry in the same way that drugs do. Anyone who has experienced love knows how consuming these feelings can be. You can think of little else. These are the emotions that give rise to appeals of addiction among collectors.

Unbridled passion has a downside. Family fortunes have been squandered, loved ones ignored and crimes committed in the name of collecting. But are we talking addiction, poor judgment or antisocial behavior? For coin collectors, the quest to complete sets, upgrade specimens, discover new die varieties, and compete in auctions sometimes can, and does, spin out of control.

To label these lapses as symptomatic of addiction is to suggest that coins somehow are similar to chemical substances in stimulating biochemical rewards and shaping our priorities. In fact, there is no evidence that coin collecting produces enhanced dopamine or glutamate responses in the brain beyond levels typically experienced during passionate moments in our lives. It is just this kind of slack thinking that has led many researchers to protest that the concept of addiction is overused; hence, we have food addicts, television addicts, and shopping addicts.

On balance, addiction is an inadequate explanation of coin collecting. The question remains: why do coin collectors rationalize their behavior by appealing to something as surly as addiction? The most parsimonious answer suggests that it is a rationalization designed to soften the sharp discrepancies between the rational numismatic marketplace and the irrationality inherent in passionate collecting. After all, collectors exert much effort justifying the purchase of new coins by appealing to the Cartesian logic of the marketplace.

For example, in his 2006 book, *The Expert's Guide to Collecting and Investing in Rare Coins*, Q. David Bowers suggests putting financial incentive first and nurturing the fascination later. In a section aptly titled, "Do it for the money," he states, "Quite a few collectors are in it for the money … *later* you will become fascinated with some of the less obvious, but equally worthwhile, aspects of numismatics."

In this era in which most numismatists call themselves "collector-investors," financial return is the reigning rationalization for collecting. This ballyhooed label is a clever way to cloak numismatic passions in a veil of rationality. But many hobbyists know otherwise; they are passionate about coins and often pay dearly for that special piece, ignoring market indicators. And so they struggle to explain love, competition and over-exuberance. This is the collecting life! It belies rational explanation. No reasonable argument justifies the purchase of a worn, battered 1793 Chain cent, only to fondle it, care for it as if it were a pet, and then refuse to sell it when offered fair market price. If challenged enough by non-collectors who do not share the numismatic faith, then pleas of addiction might make them go away; after all, everyone knows something about addiction.

Instead, why not revel in the knowledge that numismatic passions stem from a constellation of exemplary human traits. Sure, our emotions get the better of us now and again, and we do not always act rationally – this, too, is only too human. In fact, neurological studies have suggested that romantic love is a biological event characterized by a cascade of dopamine flooding our reward system. In short, love is a powerful motivator that often makes us act irrationally. As collectors, we love 1909-S VDBs, brilliant uncirculated Morgans, and the glint of a double eagle. And no, we will never sell them.

So, next time someone asks why you collect coins, you might more accurately say, "Because I love them, and they bring me great joy!" After all, it is not pathological to be smitten.

After obtaining a coin, I didn't put it on display or gaze at it for days. But I did feel good, as if a terrible itch had finally been scratched. With my collection I felt a sense of order, control, even power. There's one other significant thing about collecting; it's addictive. I mean that it can become, for some, as consuming and ultimately out of control as a drug habit. Of course the out-of-control part doesn't happen for a long time. First you are swept away by your new passion. You find yourself thinking about it all the time. For me, it was a matter of constantly looking for that next acquisition and maneuvering to get it.

— *Bruce McNall with M. D'Antonio,* Fun While it Lasted: My Rise and Fall in the Land of Fame and Fortune, 2003

"With wide-eyed

enthusiasm, I left my

marbles behind."

14

Born to
Collect Coins

I was a "big pockets" collector as a youngster. Marbles were my favorite: cat's-eyes, bumble bees, and flags. I had drawers and secret boxes full of stuff saved. I was particularly enamored with my set of Wrigley gum wrappers, particularly the old paper Juicy Fruit label with green stripes (not the usual yellow). I knew it was old, and I liked to think that I had saved the only one.

One time I thought of collecting a set of red and white Campbell's soup labels; after all, there were many different ones. It was natural for me to think this way. By the time I was 9, this kink in my brain was asserting itself more often than not! I did not amuse myself with history or culture, I just noticed the differences and wanted one of each. I had inherited a collecting urge!

A predilection for collecting can start with a floor full of marbles, shells, and coins.

It was only a matter of time before I discovered coins. A single Buffalo nickel jolted me like nothing else before. With wide-eyed enthusiasm, I left my marbles behind. Sure, I was an *accidental numismatist*, but I never wavered or looked back. It was as if I was born to collect coins.

The idea that collecting coins reflects an inheritance is not new. George Pipes remarked in the December 1939 *The Numismatist* that, "Collectors are just born that way … if the germ is in the blood, it will break out sooner or later." He likened coin collecting to a more "virulent form" of the "instinct;" whereas milder symptoms included collecting "souvenir spoons or match covers." A spoon or matchbook collector would probably not agree.

Collecting has been part of human history since primitive times. Like many birds and mammals, we share a hunting and gathering heritage. Seasonal changes, famine, and siege warfare underscored the need for men to plan ahead while gathering and hoarding items essential for survival. But for some, this urge became a leisure activity. Archaeologists have discovered accumulations of shells, crystals, odd pebbles dating back to the

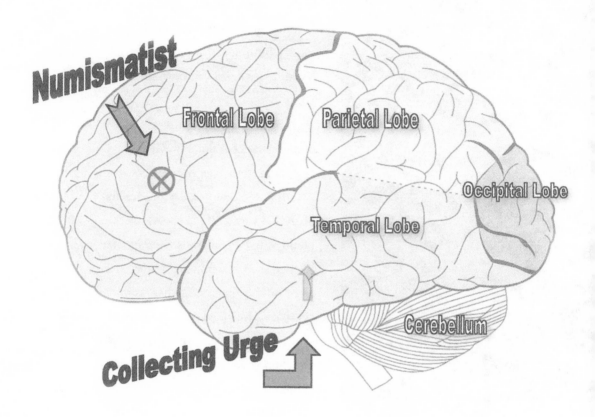

The brain of the numismatist. Unbridled collecting (and accumulation) is governed by nerves deep in the brain that have been shaped by our hunting and gathering heritage, but our interest in completing sets of Buffalo nickels or Morgan dollars resides in the frontal cortex.

Paleolithic era – these were the first collections.

Perhaps my collecting reflected this ancient heritage. I am not alone however, as surveys have suggested that collecting peaks between ages 8 and 11, with nearly 93 percent of boys and girls collecting something before the sixth grade. Marbles, like the ones I collected, were listed among the most popular items sought after – seashells and rocks were also popular. Children typically have several collections going at once, as their curiosity is unbounded and easily ignited.

Neurobiological studies have isolated several brain structures involved in collecting behavior. These networks of nerve fibers lie deep in the subcortical brain, having evolved early on. Their importance is obvious, as individuals who gathered and hoarded food were more likely to survive in times of scarcity. However, these primitive brain structures do not direct collecting toward any specific set of objects; rather, collecting at this level is indiscriminant, as my gum wrappers and soup labels attest.

In contrast, higher cortical processes govern the selection of objects. We collect what is interesting and weed out all the rest. The selection process we use is an inhibitory one. Instead of collecting all sorts of things with a big pockets mentality, the frontal cortex *reigns in* our primitive urge as we mature. Indeed, reasoning and problem solving skills take over in adulthood, and we become more choosey.

Some folks with damage to the frontal cortex have found their subcortical collecting urge unleashed. Collecting becomes haphazard, and in some cases, rampant. This is because the inhibitory function of the frontal cortex is altered or destroyed. For example, several patients who experienced frontal lobe damage exhibited irrepressible tendencies to take home pens, clips, and other small items – not to use, but just to keep.

These cases clearly locate the urge to collect in the more primitive brain regions, but suggest that this urge is inhibited, thereby controlled, by higher cortical networks in the frontal cortex. They also suggest that it would be ex-tremely rare for a brain injury to result in an increase in focused and passionate

Multiple collectors go beyond coins as their urge to collect attracts them to a wide

collecting. *An auto accident will not produce a numismatist*!

It is not surprising that children are primed to collect, as their frontal lobes are not fully developed until early adulthood. Consequently, a single item can easily spark a collecting interest. When I think about all my marbles, comics, labels, and gum wrappers, I think it must be a developmental milestone. Thomas Elder sums up the developmental process succinctly in the December 1916 issue of *The Numismatist*:

> *It will be noted that collectors of coins are not always born collectors of coins. To relate my own humble experience, I was first a collector*

variety of items; in this case, oil cans have captured the collector's imagination.

of tobacco tin-tags at 8 years, then a collector of Indian relics, then a collector of fossils. Finally, at 13, my father gave me his small coin collection, and from then my interest in coins was dated. This was a great many years ago, and I regard it was simply through accident that I became a coin collector.

Considering the neurobiological findings discussed above, it make sense that childhood collecting is so ripe with variation. Young children amass whatever objects catch their fancy without reflection or self-reproach. Furthermore, the peak of collecting around 12 years of age signals when the brain boasts its highest level of neural interconnectivity. After this age, the brain begins to prune away some of these connections, becoming more streamlined and mature. In fact, these same surveys suggest that collecting slows down after the eighth grade.

On balance, individual differences in collecting reflect underlying differences in brain physiology. These differences are of two basic types: 1) collectors can differ in the amount of collecting urge that they have – that is, brain differences can be at the subcortial level; and 2) collectors can differ in their interests. In the latter case, we know that learning and experience have a tremendous impact in determining what the collector will choose to pursue.

As with all attributes in life, a few folks are likely to have a weak collecting urge, whereas an equally small group will have a powerful collecting urge. Most will fall in the middle zone with a moderate collecting urge. The same is true for collecting interests, perhaps best characterized, as "how much restraint or selectivity" is shown when pursuing desired objects like Buffalo nickels.

At the high end of the collecting spectrum we find the *multiple collectors*. They are the ones that have several collections going at once (well into adulthood). Dr. Edward Maris, known for his classification of New Jersey coppers also collected autographs. The author of the acclaimed, *Early Coins of America*, Sylvester Crosby, collected artifacts from archaeological digs. Prolific numismatic author and collector Q. David Bowers has collected coin-operated music boxes for decades. These illustrious numismatists collected many things other than coins; they had a strong urge!

So it seems that some folks are destined to be collectors. They chose coins through serendipity, but they would have found something else to collect if events had been different. This is the collecting "instinct" as it were: the consequence of a more developed, more sensitive, subcortical collecting center located deep in the brain. Hence, we unexpectedly stumble onto coins. *We are all accidental numismatists.*

David Lange, author of *Coin Collecting Boards of the 1930s & 1940s*, provides a vignette that highlights how events can spark coin collecting in those who already possess a predilection to collect. When Richard Yeo (R.S. Yeoman)

The *America the Beautiful* series could spark the collecting urge in children.

brought the newfangled coin boards to his office at Whitman Publishing, he noticed, "… how fellow employees began taking them home to try their luck at filling them." He likened it to completing a crossword puzzle, and it seemed like "everyone had to fill that last hole in their penny boards." The public had a similar reaction; collecting cents became all the rage. From the novelty of filling in the holes, many *born-to-be* collectors were introduced to numismatics.

This "release" of latent collecting behavior is paralleled by the public reaction to all sorts of collecting schemes used in advertising promotions, from the Shell Oil presidential coins of the 1960s to collectible toys given out with fast foods. The publication of a guidebook can transform ordinary playthings into a series of collectibles: Matchbox cars, Barbie dolls, and G.I Joes. The subcortical urge to collect is harnessed by the rational frontal cortex to complete the set, once interest is stimulated.

It makes good sense to spark the collecting urge in children under 12 by introducing coin boards and describing set completion strategies. The *50 State quarters* and *America the Beautiful* series are ripe with novelty while providing just enough challenge to keep kids hunting for those coins that are still missing from the set. In addition, there are many colorful albums and guidebooks available to entice children to read more about the coins thereby stimulating numismatic interests.

As these interests develop, young numismatists can be taught to search for better specimens that upgrade the set. In addition, the series are ripe with die varieties that lend themselves to young inquisitive eyes – for example extra leaves on 2004 Wisconsin corn stalks and doubled trees on 2005 Minnesota hilltops. Such challenges come naturally to the born collector! Just as many of us old-timers recall looking for 1909-S VDB cents, the thrill of treasure hunting is alive and well today. And with nearly a half-century of coins still in circulation, this is no time for adults to lament that the *good old days* have passed.

Yes, the collecting urge is alive and well. Sometimes, I gaze in the mirror trying to figure it out; I ponder the collecting kink in my brain, as if I could actually see it in my face somewhere. I know that I am not alone. We are all fortunate to have discovered coins and the numismatic fraternity – I am not so sure that soup labels would have provided the same rewards. Yet, I still feel the urge to collect every time I envision a set of objects, no matter how arcane. Are you this way? I hope so, because to collect whatever captures your fancy (without self-reproach) is one of the true joys of numismatics!

The collecting urge is often triggered in the nursery by the arrival of an unexpected present or by a particular experience: the gift of a foreign doll, perhaps, or a visit to a museum. Children are often obsessive collectors, whether of conkers, lead soldiers, Dinky toys, or coins ... sometimes this early excitement can develop into a lifelong interest ... sometimes it can dominate the entire life of the collector and become an academic absorption.

— *Susanna Johnston*, Collecting: The Passionate Pastime, 1986

"They have been around

longer and come from

places that look, smell, and

taste different."

Getting Started: Collecting the Whole World

One of the memorable tasks at the end of the family summer vacation was to choose a sticker that proclaimed: *We were there – Grand Canyon, Chicago, Virginia Beach*. These flashy logos with rounded block letters and cartoon sketches of cliffs, skyscrapers, and surfboards vied for tailgate space. It was a collage of images meant to take us back. As a collector, I mostly remember the agony of choosing just one. Should I get the surfboard or the lighthouse?

World coins are about images. We do not have to visit the place – the images are in our heads and on the coins. In this age of digital saturation, we have been everywhere at all times. We have witnessed the birth of a Panda in China; we have watched a royal scandal unfold in England – all in the comfort of our easy chair. We also have witnessed the fall of Rome and traveled on Spanish galleons with pirates closing in. Foreign coins stir our imaginations in similar ways: exotic animals, regalia, and centuries of history. Like those colorful logos, world coins transport us. And we do not have to choose just one!

A few years ago I decided that I wanted to explore the coins that circulated in the American colonies – money that foretold the shape of things to come. I purchased a Spanish colonial Pillar dollar dated 1744. It was a crusty old coin with a pea-green  taint that came with a sea-salvage certificate. This venerable coin hailed from a Dutch East Indiaman – "Reijgersdaal" – that floundered in October of 1747 during a gale off the southern tip of Africa.

The ship broke up on the rocks, and the crew – riddled with scurvy – was unable to do anything but watch the hull disintegrate into sharp splinters. Only a few sailors survived. Eight chests, containing nearly 30,000 coins, sunk to the bottom. My coin had witnessed it all; I was holding a piece of the action. I started to read about sailing ships, world trade, and the empires of the Dutch and the Spanish. This coin had transported me to a whole new world of images.

This piece of eight was intriguing in other ways too. It is the first coin pictured in the *Guide Book of United States Coins* (or *Red Book*) where it was described as a "time-honored piece" that "has been given a place in romantic fiction unequaled by any other coin." Pirates, patriots, and peddlers all depended on the coin with "two sticks" as the Chinese merchants liked to call it. The pillars symbolized the straits of Gibraltar flanking two globes representing the east and west hemispheres of the planet: a symbol of Spain's imperialistic claim to the new world across the Atlantic.

I subsequently developed an interest in Spanish colonialism and the great treasure fleets loaded with silver that sailed out of Havana in the late summer. Many of these colonial coins circulated in the great cities of Atlanta, Baltimore, New York, and Boston. In fact, Spanish milled dollars traded as legal tender in the United States until 1857. I had found a new passion that led me around the world yet kept me grounded to my homeland where the coins were familiar.

This is what world coins can do for the collector. They have been around

World coins are about images – real or imagined – of places that look, smell, and taste different. This German 5-mark coin shows a stylized eagle quite unlike any found on American coins.

longer and come from places that look, smell, and taste different. They are completely novel and complex but can be readily understood with medium effort if we can find the right connections. As one writer opined in the October 1964 issue of *The Numismatist*: "A thousand collectors can choose a thousand different lines, because numismatics has an answer for everybody ... whatever your personal interest, you will find it mirrored on coins." He, too, was looking beyond our shores.

Still, American collectors often struggle to make the leap into world coins. We are familiar with cents and dollars, not pesos, euros, or rupees. If you were to wander over to the far side of a large bourse where the foreign coin dealers congregate, your initial reaction is likely to be one of confusion. The variety of coins offered can be mind-boggling. Where do you start?

Many collectors start off by exploring a few coins from the "old country" where a great grandparent was raised. We all came from somewhere else. Besides, some of us just need a logical reason to take that first step. Once a few coins are examined, we are likely to discover that the motifs found on world coins are quite interesting. There are many stunning designs out there that provide a welcomed retreat from the staleness that has characterized more than a few American coin series. Imagine: coins without presidents, buildings, and eagles!

Foreign mints have invigorated the field of metallic art in recent years. In fact, many European nations – Austria provides a prolific example – have gained a reputation for producing exquisitely detailed commemorative coins that have become popular with collectors for their beauty and exclusivity. In a more blatant attempt to capture the interest of collectors, a growing number of foreign mints have unveiled fine art pieces that depict events of interest to all humanity ranging from the Olympics to space exploration to exotic beasts. Even Elvis Presley has been honored on coins from far away places like the Cook Islands in the Pacific – maybe this is where he has been hiding all these years!

In addition to producing great art, world coins have become quite innovative. The Pobjoy Mint produced a titanium coin for Gibraltar in 2000

This bi-metallic 10-euro coin from Austria has a blue niobium center.

that aptly celebrated the start of the new millennium. Once reserved for space shuttles and competition mountain bikes, this expensive element has become rather common in numismatics. Not to be upstaged, the Austrian mint introduced a bimetallic 10-euro piece with a deep-blue niobium center in 2003 marking the 700th anniversary of one of its oldest cities; subsequent issues have purple and green niobium centers produced by heat-treating this exotic metal. Other niobium coins have been produced for far-flung places like Mongolia and Sierra Leone.

Canada introduced a colorized quarter in 2000 to celebrate its national heritage; this technology applied translucent red ink to highlight the maple leaf emblem on the flag! In 2004, this process was adapted for the first time for "poppy" quarters minted for circulation in remembrance of those who lost their lives during military action. This colorized coinage was described as the "most innovative circulation coin" at a worldwide Mint directors' conference later that year. Canada has continued to innovate by attaching tanzanite crystals to produce sparkling snowflake designs for the collector market in 2010.

Other countries have produced colorized versions of their own with more realistic images: imagine a great white shark swimming right at you on Palau's 2010 one dollar coin. Clearly, the mints of the world have recognized that the coin collector market is eager for innovation! It is up to you to decide how far to go with all of this, as numismatic art is well on the way toward blending sculpture with imaging – not at all surprising in an increasingly digital world!

These numismatic delicacies aside, one of the most enduring aspects of world coins is the broad range of affordable collecting options stretching back to antiquity. Circulating coins often trade at close to face value, and mail-order dealers routinely sell minor world coins by the pound or by the hundreds. If you are wondering about ancient or medieval coins, they can be had for as low as five dollars apiece for crusty, but detailed enough, specimens. Imagine holding a copper *quadrans* from Rome and wondering if it was spent to buy a freshly baked loaf at the forum – I wonder what barley bread tasted like 2000 years ago?

No matter how one is introduced to world coins, it is only a matter of time before the coins take over, and our dabbling becomes serious. Our set completion urges get the upper hand, as we begin to explore our options. My own experiences have shown that some dalliances are inevitable, as there are so many historic, beautiful, and innovative coins to choose from. But eventually, we decide on a tentative plan: pursue a type set, develop an aesthetic theme, or complete a series.

Forming a type set from a particular country or region is the traditional route. One popular way to manage the diversity is to start with a well-defined series; for example, many collectors like to explore Europe with euros. First issued in 2002, each coin is of identical size and composition and shares a common obverse, giving unity to the set. But the reverse designs uniquely reflect the heritage of the member countries. Some of the euro designs are quite attractive: Finland's euros show two flying swans; those from Greece depict an ancient Athenian owl. The collector can choose to focus on just the 1 and 2-euro coins, or a complete set of fractional coins as well. As mentioned above, commemorative coin programs are extremely popular and promise to extend the set indefinitely.

Trade coins represent a fascinating collecting specialty, particularly when they come from shipwrecks: (from left to right at bottom) French Ecu from the "Chameau" sunk off Nova Scotia in 1725; a Dutch Ducaton (or "leg dollar") from unknown sea salvage; Dutch Leeuwendaalder (or "lion dollar") salvaged from the "Campen" sunk in 1627 in the English channel; Dutch Rijksdaalder from unknown sea salvage; Dutch Ducatoon (or "silver rider") from the "Hollandia" sunk in 1743 off the southwest coast of England; Spanish Netherlands Ducatoon salvaged from the "Slot ter Hooge" sunk in 1724 northwest of Africa; and English Crown salvaged from the "Association" sunk in 1707 off the west coast of England.

If older coins are desired, the euro set can be extended to include the denominations that came before. In this case, the collector needs to be prepared to cope with a wide variety of metals, shapes, and sizes. Trying to make sense of differences in monetary systems is a fascinating endeavor that can lead in many directions. To think that the Italian *lira* dates back to the seventh century and is derived from the Latin word *libra*, referring to a measure of weight (in this case, a Roman pound) puts monetary units into a practical perspective. This is but one of the journeys that old coins can lead you on.

Another broad but manageable collecting focus can be organized around an empire such as the British domains at the turn of the 19th century. Coins of the Commonwealth span several continents and include: South Africa, India, Australia, and New Zealand, not to mention many small isles like the Bahamas and Jamaica. Most of these coins can be collected in the pre-decimal system of pence, shillings and pounds. Like euros, they share similar obverse designs – in this case, depicting the royal monarch of the era. This unity makes collecting within a specific denomination attractive: collecting "crowns" or 5-shilling coins is particularly popular, as the coins are big, full of silver, and feature many commemorative designs.

Big pocket collectors who want to combine collecting with investment in silver or gold bullion have found that world coins offer some of the best opportunities to form interesting

◀ This coin has traveled around the world and bears the chop marks of Chinese merchants to prove it. Spanish pillar dollars, such as this one, are popular among collectors, as they are inexpensive and have great stories to tell.

sets. In fact, hundreds of gold coins – both modern and classic – are traded at prices slightly over bullion values. One popular strategy is to collect European 20-franc coins and their equivalents; these relatively inexpensive coins contain a fifth of an ounce of gold providing some solace for the investor. For the more adventurous who want the challenge of deciphering Arabian script, this series can be easily extended to Middle Eastern trade coins of similar content that date back to the middle-ages. Finally, a wide variety of ducats can be added to this collection – some of them dating back to the 13th century!

For the gold bug who is attracted to uniformity in design and wants a series to collect, British sovereigns offer a broad scope, as they have been minted regularly from 1817 in far-flung mints as Sydney, Melbourne, Perth, Ottawa, Bombay, Pretoria, and of course, London. The common reverse design depicting Saint George slaying the dragon is dramatically beautiful and steeped in legend. With nearly a quarter-ounce of gold content, these coins are quite a bit larger than ducats and represent a store of value while offering the collector multiple challenges of forming sets that mix or match monarchs and mints.

Perhaps the most adventurous route for the world coin collector is to develop a collecting theme that traverses time and culture. Topical collecting is the wildest frontier in numismatics, as guidebooks are few and set definition is wide open. Animals and plants are particularly popular, as the choices are nearly infinite. With so many options to choose from, the collector

Spanish colonial trade coins represent a fascinating area of collecting that provides a gateway into the dangerous world of pirates and shipwrecks.

can form a virtual menagerie of exotic beasts with world coins. Even dinosaurs grace the surface of some coins whereas ancient coins feature mythical beasts.

With the whole world at your disposal, a bountiful collection can be formed that just focuses on fish, birds, or some other specific animal group. This kind of aesthetic collecting can be shaped around non-numismatic interests as well: fish for the angler! In this regard, one world coin retailer has labeled its catalog a "Coin Aquarium." Here you can catch fish without bothering with grimy worms or expensive lures. How about a starfish? You can find them on circulating one-cent pieces from the Bahamas! Certainly, this can be a collection that kids, and even dispassionate houseguests, can enjoy.

For the historian who wants to go topical, world coins offer a literal glimpse into the past. I once met a collector of medieval castles and cityscapes. He proudly showed me a meticulously detailed walled city on a German *thaler* (a dollar-sized silver coin) dated 1633 – it was one of the most spectacular pieces I had ever seen. He spent more time searching than acquiring, but the long hunts were worth the excitement of discovering a new place, its image lost to history except for a single coin. He was a discoverer of lost cities!

Despite the pull of distant lands and diverse images, Canadian and Mexican coins have remained extremely popular due to their proximity to the United States. Consequently, several guidebooks have combined these series; for example, David Harper has edited a three-in-one guidebook entitled, *North American Coins & Prices,* that includes listings for the whole continent. This merger reflects broader trends in multiculturalism that some say is overdue among American collectors. Besides, our neighbors offer ample choices for indulging in type and series collecting pursuits that we find familiar.

It should not be surprising that Canadian coins are popular with American collectors. Canada has used cents and dollars for as long as any of us can

Canadian silver coins form a beautiful series with naturalistic designs.

remember and shares our history of French and English colonization. The coins are at once familiar and are sometimes found in our own pocket change. Coin folders for Canadian series are readily available and invite collectors to complete date sets. I once collected three-fourths of a folder of Maple Leaf cents over the course of a weekend business conference in Vancouver; I enjoyed the ride just as I had with my Lincoln cents during my formative years.

Unlike the United States, Canada issued large cents from 1858 until 1920 and silver 5-cent pieces from 1837 to 1921 – such disparities entice collectors who want something different, but not too spicy. Another enticement for *going Canadian* is the beauty of their naturalistic designs: a maple leaf, beaver, or caribou – these are refreshing symbols that capture the splendor of this vast country composed mostly of open frontier and fauna. If you want to be "green" or go organic, then this is the coinage for you!

Canadian silver dollars, minted from 1935 to 1967, represent a very collectible series made more interesting with commemorative designs appearing about every 10 years (in 1935, 1949, 1958 and 1967). The voyageur design – a fur trader and Indian guide rowing a canoe together – is pleasing and captures the heritage and natural beauty of the country. In addition, there are a few challenging rarities plus numerous die varieties that invite specialization for those handy with a magnifying glass. The circulating series ends with the iconic 1867-1967 Confederation Centennial dollar whose lone goose is chastely rendered, wings extended-down in flight. In recent years, the Royal Canadian Mint has produced commemorative silver dollars annually – including colorized and bimetallic pieces – providing collectors with more than enough coins to fill stockings at the end of the year.

For the collector who ventures south of the border, Spanish Colonial and Mexican coins offer the challenge of completing long sets of silver coins dating back to the 1530s. In particular, Spanish Colonial milled dollars, minted from 1732 to 1772 (Pillar dollars) and 1773 to 1820 (Portrait dollars) provide a series that the average collector with medium budget can complete in the upper circulated grades. These pieces of eight were widely traded among merchants in the North American colonies and are considered to be the forerunners of our own silver dollars.

The Cap and Ray coins, first produced in 1823, that marked Mexican independence are also readily available. The series spans a tumultuous 19th century and is ripe with overdates, design variations, mints, and assayer marks. These large silver coins are impressive and affordable offering great appeal to the full pockets collector who enjoys the sparkle of silver. Even a type set of 1, 2, 4 and 8 reales including the early transitional designs of 1823 would be challenging to complete with all the subtypes and mints represented. These coins often found their way into the United States territories, passing as silver bullion, before mints were established west of the Mississippi. In addition, they circulated widely on the world trade market.

North of the border, south of the border, or across the seas, world coins offer many opportunities to escape. Like traveling out into the countryside, the hustle of crowds is left behind. Consequently, prices are more reasonable. Also, the anxiety associated with grading is reduced somewhat, as world coin markets are driven more by their diversity than by an obsessive concern about condition and value. It has often been reported that European collectors, for instance, are more concerned about getting a "good enough" example for their collections, than getting the "best available" specimen.

Consequently, the United States collector who dabbles, or even defects, to world coins can breathe a sigh of relief, as the marketplace ticks along at a slower, less pressured pace. One of the things I have enjoyed about my Spanish Colonial coins is that there are many interesting coins to choose from without the urgency of having to act fast, or bid exorbitantly, to get nice coins that fit into the collection. Few of these coins are slabbed, and they look great in circulated condition, in part, because the design motifs are ornate and rival the best eagles, wreaths, and figures found on United States coins. After all, it is all about the images: on the coins and in our heads.

"The manner in which

collected objects

assuage the anxieties

associated with loss is

truly 'magical.'"

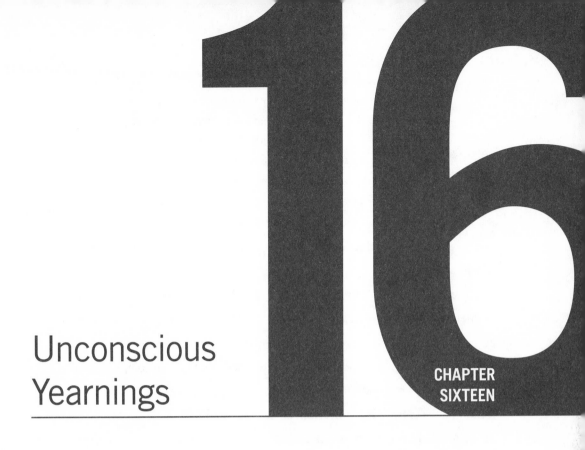

Unconscious Yearnings

Sigmund Freud was passionate about antiquities. He started collecting sculptural objects from Rome, Greece, and Egypt in the late 1890s. By the 1920s, he had broadened his scope, acquiring a variety of rings, masks, and scarabs; he also nurtured an interest in Middle-Eastern and Chinese artifacts as he grew older. At the time of his death in September 1939, he had amassed over 3,000 pieces. His acquisition strategy was eclectic, as each piece was judged by its historic merits without considering its role in the collection as a whole.

His objects sometimes overshadowed the great analyst himself as revealed in a particularly poignant vignette, provided by one of Freud's patients upon entering the consulting room for the first time (quoted by John Forrester in his essay, *"Mille etre:" Freud and Collecting*):

> *I walk through the door. It closes. Sigmund Freud does not speak …*
> *I look around the room. Pricelessly lovely objects are displayed here*
> *on the shelves to right, to the left … no one told me that this room was*

lined with treasures. I was to greet the Old Man of the Sea, but no
one had told me of the treasures he had salvaged from the sea-depth
... waiting and finding that I would not or could not speak, he uttered
... "You are the only person who has ever come into this room and
looked at the things in the room before looking at me."

Indeed, patients lying on the venerable "therapy" couch would find themselves besieged by vestiges of the ages – a fitting metaphor for the process of psychoanalysis.

The intensity of Freud's passion was revealed in a letter to his close friend, Wilhelm Fliess: "I have sacrificed a great deal for my collection ... [and] have actually read more archaeology than psychology." Freud's communion with his beloved objects was transparent and unabashed. For example, Freud often brought newly acquired sculptures to his dining table to enjoy during meals. He fondled objects from his collection, as he consulted with patients. On occasion, Freud greeted his favorite pieces with "Good morning" at the start of the day. Yet, with a curious humility, Freud would often refer to the collection as his "old and filthy gods."

There are parallels between Freud's collecting and his psychodynamic theorizing. As Forrester noted, "Freud's desire to be an archaeologist of the mind was a long-standing feature of his inner life." The methodology of psychoanalysis wherein fragments of memory, affect, and cognition are unearthed via free association and pieced together to tell a coherent story of personality development is similar to that of the archaeologist. Both the psychoanalyst and the archaeologist are collectors of history. In his work, Freud collected many case studies, dreams, and slips-of-the-tongue in an effort to uncover the unconscious workings of the mind.

One of Freud's earliest comments on collecting captures the essence of classic psychodynamic thinking. In 1895, again writing to his friend and colleague, Wilhelm Fliess, he opined:

When an old maid keeps a dog or an old bachelor collects snuffboxes,
the former is finding a substitute for a companion in marriage and

Sigmund Freud in 1926. He was an avid collector of antiquities, once remarking that he had read more about archeology than psychology.
© LIFE photo archive

the latter for his need for – a multitude of conquests. Every collector is a substitute for a Don Juan Tenerio.

In short, coin collecting was viewed as a coping strategy born out of frustration and loss. And like all unresolved unconscious conflicts, the act of collecting is destined to repeat itself over and over again. For the neophyte, psychoanalytic formulations appear to suggest that collecting is akin to psychopathology. This is unfortunate, as these theories are rich in detail and deepen our understanding of how negative events can shape collecting.

Psychoanalyst Werner Muensterberger has likened the act of collecting to a coping strategy in his book *Collecting: An Unruly Passion*:

> *Whatever the motivation, there is little question that collecting is much more than the simple experience of pleasure. If that were the case, one butterfly, or one painting, would be enough. Instead, repetition is mandatory. Repeated acquisitions serve as a vehicle*

to cope with inner anxiety, with confusing problems of need and longing.

Consequently, a single coping response is never quite adequate, as the collecting must continue to sustain the transitory feelings of comfort that come with acquisition.

The manner in which collected objects assuage the anxieties associated with loss is truly "magical." The collection is imbued with the power to heal old wounds while protecting against new ones. In this regard, Peter Subkowski, writing in the *International Journal of Psychoanalysis* suggested that this magic stems from the coping strategies often used by children who use transitional objects – a blanket, Teddy bear, or favorite toy – to provide security when mother or father are away:

> *These objects, over which full control may be exerted, help the child to better cope with separation. The transitional object also allows one to forget a lost and/or unrequited love. The collector, too, can unconsciously defend against fear of loss by displacing relationship needs to an animated object with which he does not wish to part.*

The transitional objects of childhood fuel the urge to collect later on. They provide a sense of control and stability in an uncontrollable world. Objects of childhood are imbued with magic, as these things have sustained us through difficult times.

Subkowski described a case study of a lonely book collector during the course of 600 one-hour sessions of psychoanalysis. He suffered dyslexia in elementary school and was "declared stupid" by his mother, giving rise to feelings of inadequacy. He subsequently developed an interest in collecting rare books about political figures. Subkowski described the patient's collecting as a "narcissistic filling" wherein bibliomania "enabled him to compensate for the defect of dyslexia and related feelings of injury and insufficiency."

A pattern developed such that failed relationships were met with a passionate quest for rare books. In the course of analysis the anger and frustration that

Coins have served a protective role throughout history. Often a silver coin was nailed to the house frame to bring prosperity and good health to the family.

the patient felt became clear. His descriptions of the intoxicant impact of new acquisitions were bristling: [with a new book in hand] "he felt grandiose and extraordinary, as if he had written it himself ... [and] imagining how his former classmates might be failing today."

The story had a happy ending. As psychoanalysis continued, the lonely bibliophile began to display a more relaxed attitude toward his books. Whereas before, his collecting was devoid of pleasant affect, he began to appear more at ease and willing to share his enthusiasm for politics beyond the mere collecting of books. His mood was brighter. He entertained the idea of seeking out new relationships. The successful outcome did not involve the repudiation of collecting; rather, his love of books became more fully integrated into his personality and no longer stood in the way of developing other parts of his life. Nonetheless, the symbolism of a dyslexic, and ridiculed, child becoming a rare book collector is inescapable.

The case of the disgruntled adult bibliophile suggests that the choice of the collected object can be highly symbolic. Psychoanalyst Werner Muensterberger does not agree that the symbolic relationship is necessary, as any number of comfort objects from childhood could become objects of desire:

> Preferences and taste are under the influence of prevailing trends and environmental conditions, especially as one grows older. Still, despite all possible variations, there is reason to believe that the true source of the [collecting] habit is the emotional state leading to a more or less perpetual attempt to surround oneself with magically potent objects.

It is likely that both scenarios are true, as each case is unique. In some situations the symbolic nature of the objects collected are clear; whereas in other circumstances, the items collected are shaped more by external factors.

It is impossible to determine the precise symbolism associated with coin collecting without exploring the intimate circumstances of each collector. The symbolic possibilities are many. A penchant for silver dollars could stem from the pangs of childhood poverty or could have been shaped by a desire to compete with a domineering father who carried a large pocket piece. So too, a robust coin like the silver dollar, heavy and full of value, might reflect stability and permanence in the face of a chaotic upbringing characterized by multiple relocations and losses. A common thread cutting across these scenarios is that the coins confer power to its owner. Each silver dollar is imbued with magical properties of the most basic kind: *they protect!*

Freud viewed magic as a psychological phenomenon designed to control uncertainty. That special coins can fill the collector with feelings of security and confidence is the substance of magic. It is a form of *animism* wherein people view non-human objects as inhabited by powerful entities. From a psychoanalytic perspective, the magic of collecting is a coping mechanism.

In addition to providing refuge from feelings of loss and longing, magical objects can also provide a bulwark against future threats of abandonment and hurt. By inflating the sense of self, the collector insulates against future adversities. This is a preemptive strategy. In addition to providing relief, acquisition of a new object is empowering. As Werner Muensterberger described (in reference to a sea shell collector):

> *Collecting is one of those defenses that promises temporary relief and brings new vitality because every new object effectively gives the notion of fantasized omnipotence. … the object becomes a countermeasure to insecurity and thus a protective narcissistic shield. It also conveys the owner's covert need to hear pronouncements of praise and admiration: "Admire the shell, which is me."*

Similarly, we can imagine the unconscious yearnings of the numismatist, "Admire the 1804 dollar, which is me!" *The collection becomes the collector.* Indeed, as psychoanalyst Scott Schwartz remarked in the *Journal of the American Academy of Psychoanalysis*, "The quality and rarity of our possessions is a sure sign of our quality and rarity as connoisseurs, as well as our strength and conquest over competitors for rare objects." With each acquisition, the collector is further, if only temporarily, insulated from the insecurities of life.

The fleeting quality of magic is clearly illustrated by observing how rare coins tend to "circulate" among collectors. Since collecting is a coping response, repeated acquisition is critical to keep the magic going. Consider the Louis Eliasberg specimen of the 1913 Liberty nickel: it has sold four times (1996, 2001, 2003, 2005) in the past 15 years. Only Eliasberg himself kept the coin for over five years. Was the lowly nickel unloved by later owners? Not hardly! They all revered it with one owner claiming the 1913 Liberty nickel to be "the Van Gogh of numismatics." It last sold for $4.1 million!

Magic apparently has a short half-life. The magic fades over time prompting the collector to sell. From a psychodynamic perspective, each collector siphons out all the magic and then passes the coin on. Call it speculating if you must, but psychoanalysts will not agree. Rather it is the nature of magical totems whose power, like novelty and the element of surprise, is evanescent. Hence, the "circulation" of numismatic rarities reflects the wax and wane of magic.

Coin collectors bolster their social status with magical objects. For example, possessing a rarity is the sign of a winner! As Schwartz notes, "… to be sure, the very personal ability to derive pleasure and pride from a beautiful acquisition" is part of the equation; but he goes on to remark that "… but rarely is a collector not stimulated by the envy and admiration of others." A favorite folktale in numismatics involves J. V. McDermott, a vest-pocket trader, who enjoyed surprising others by pulling out some loose change in his pocket and pointing out the 1913 Liberty nickel that he was carrying around. He passed it around all the while beaming with pride.

This script is played out over and over again by collectors at coin club meetings, conventions, and on the auction floor. Everyone is posturing to express their numismatic self. Each script is unique: flashing rarities, sporting a unique loupe, toting thick texts, jotting notes on an auction catalog. The procession is wholly idiosyncratic and hard to decipher, as each collector reaches for his idealized self while fanning the feathers for all to see.

The notion of the ideal self should not be surprising in a consumer-based economy where marketing strategies target the image-conscious and the all-too-human desire to inflate one's ego. Social psychologist Helga Dittmar has

With only five specimens known, the 1913 Liberty nickel is considered to be one of the most prestigious prizes in coin collecting. Such status imbues the coin with magical powers enough to elevate anyone who possesses it to the exalted status of numismatic connoisseur *par excellence*.

described two ways that possessions pump up their owners in the *Journal of Social Behavior and Personality*:

> *A highly significant dimension of material objects is that they serve as symbolic expressions of who we are. As categorical symbols, they can signify status and the broad social categories we belong to, but also the smaller groups we identify with. Self-expressive functions concern individuals' unique attitudes, goals, and personality qualities. What we accumulate during our lifetime comes to represent our personal history and relationships.*

We are surrounded by these symbols and we actively choose many of them. Yet, it is important to recognize that these symbols cut deeply into our psyche and come from places deep in the unconscious mind.

Consequently, collectors are not immediately aware of all the determinants of their passion. For at its core, the psychoanalytic perspective considers the collecting urge to be a defense mechanism designed to protect the ego. Again, psychoanalyst Werner Muensterberger noted that collecting has the "the aim of turning disillusionment and helplessness into an animated, purposeful venture." His view sharply disagrees with the romantic impression that coin collecting is sparked by some fortuitous discovery of a marvelous coin – no, as psychoanalysts would have it, deeply rooted, unconscious impulses were in play long before.

Lest the reader become concerned that the psychoanalytic tradition paints a negative view of the collecting life, it is important to recognize that all people have experienced frustration and loss. As such, all people use defense mechanisms of some kind to cope. Psychoanalysts largely agree that collecting can be a mature and fulfilling activity that contributes to healthy adult functioning. It is only when collecting dominates life and threatens to interfere with one's ability to work, love, and play that the pursuit is considered pathological. Rather, collecting provides many intellectual, emotional, and social benefits in a world full of hurts.

Having something desirable creates security and strength, while lacking or envying creates gaping lacunae. This universal human attribute spans all societies and belief systems. Therefore, we all collect. We collect knowledge, we collect techniques, we collect honors and degrees, we collect clothes and shoes, we collect experiences, we even collect friends. There is nothing cheap or tawdry about feeling safe with what we can rely on as being ours.

— *Scott C. Schwartz, M.D., Fellow and trustee of the American Academy of Psychoanalysis,* Journal of the American Academy of Psychoanalysis, December 2001

"Sometimes numismatics

becomes a unifying

family pastime or a

matter of ancestral

heritage."

Immortality
Striving

CHAPTER SEVENTEEN

Massachusetts cents, several "horse and plow" coppers from New Jersey, a stack of misshapen counterfeit George III half-pence, a clipped cob from Potosi, and miscellaneous pillars, portraits, and pistareens – an 18th-century mercantile collection assembled by a colonial coin collector. Perhaps a similar cache existed in an old Philadelphia shop. I am having fun on a cloudy afternoon.

This selection reflects an idea. Not so much history in my hand, but history in my head. The collection is alive. These colonials are an intimate part of me. The assemblage is uniquely my own. *Who else will appreciate what I have done?*

The coin collection is an extension of the collector. As Susan Pearce commented in *Museums, Objects, and Collections: A Cultural Study*, "Collections are endowed with a life of their own, which bears the most intimate relationship to that of the collector, so that the collector sees them, in the most literal sense, as parts of himself." Survival of the collection is survival of

A fanciful assemblage of 18th century coins that reflects an historical idea in the collector's head. Who will appreciate what I have done on this tabletop? Who will appreciate the planning and effort to capture my image of a historical moment with coins?

the self. There is a direct connection between the permanence of the collection and the immortality of the collector. Russell Belk noted in *Collectors and Collecting*, "… having lived through the collection … the collector's desire for immortality through the collection is not surprising."

The final disposition of the collection – this life project – is a serious affair. The measure of the collector is at stake here. We pose the ultimate question: *Who else will appreciate what I have done?* From a museum curator's point of view, Susan Pearce notes that collectors are "extremely anxious that a collection will not be split up" and that some pieces will go unappreciated. This anxiety is sharpened when one considers the history of each coin: some represent heirlooms collected by one's forefathers; others were obtained after protracted searching and negotiating; still other pieces represent seminal finds that shaped all that was collected thereafter. How can an heir possibly know these important facts?

There are several ways that a collection can continue into the afterlife. The most prestigious route is for the collection to be accepted into a museum. The more popular the museum, the better! I can imagine my modest cache of colonial coins spilling from an over-filled cash drawer placed on a counter's desk in an exhibit of a portside customs house in Philadelphia.

What better way to immortalize what I have done!

Pearce notes how the collector's desire for recognition dovetails with the curator's own acquisitive quest whereby the objects are transformed in the process:

> ... the collector's desire for immortality is so strong, and the curator's desire to acquire interesting material so fierce, that a fairly satisfactory agreement is reached surprisingly frequently. If entry into a collection is an object's first rite of passage, then entry into a museum is its second – a passage that marks its translation into the class of heritage material, of sacred durables.

To be credited with selecting such important coins – *heritage material* – is a high honor. The collector's desire for immortality plus the wish to show reverence for the coins themselves are satisfied.

Many prominent numismatists have been immortalized in museum collections. In the 1920s, Farren Zerbe donated his extensive collection of world coins to form the nucleus of the *Chase Manhattan Bank Money Museum*. As an added benefit, he served as the curator for several years. The collection was eventually absorbed into the *Smithsonian National Money Collection*. The collection of rare gold, pattern coinage, and silver certificates assembled by Harry W. Bass has been immortalized in the *American Numismatic Association Money Museum* at Colorado Springs. Eric P. Newman's esteemed collection of colonial coins and Benjamin Franklin items found residence at the *Newman Money Museum* at Washington University in St. Louis, Mo.

Another option for preserving collections is to establish a "cottage" museum. These are memorials, as they are often named after the collector. An endowment is often attached, and the museum solicits donations to pay operating costs. Sometimes surviving family members serve as curators. If the museum is popular enough, admission fees might supplement family income. When a home cannot be found, the collection might "travel" as a special exhibit to local history museums or community libraries during Founders Week or the Fourth of July. Communities are grateful for these collections.

A collector may encourage heirs to continue a collection. This can be tricky, as collecting is a very personal endeavor. Consequently, finding family members who share the passion can be difficult. Nonetheless, it does happen. Sometimes numismatics becomes a unifying family pastime or a matter of ancestral heritage. In his book *The History of United States Coinage Illustrated by the Garrett Collection*, Q. David Bowers described the collecting spirit that was passed from father to sons in the Garrett family. T. Harrison Garrett's collection of United States coinage was first taken up by his youngest son, Robert Garrett, but later became the focus of enthusiastic expansion under the tutelage of John Work Garrett. The collection spanned nearly 80 years of collecting between the 1860s and 1940s.

A potential heir to the collection may need grooming to stimulate interest. Russell Belk described such a case in *Collectors and Collecting*,

> … *the collector of elephant replicas … plans to leave the entire collection to his granddaughter, although she was only a year old. He has already given her several elephant toys (he says he is making a point of it) as well as an elephant print dress.*

Young numismatists search to fill Lincoln
Memorial cent folders at ANA. This is the
future of coin collecting.

Belk goes on to say that this collector "wants to believe that his collection is historically important and that people will some day appreciate what he has accomplished." The significance of collecting as an extension of the self that reflects one's life accomplishment is clear.

Like the elephant replica collector, coin collectors encourage the development of numismatic interests in children. Parents give their children proof sets and Lincoln cent folders. Coin shows typically offer a *Young Numismatist* table hosting introductory learning forums and "treasure hunt" activities. These efforts aim to cultivate a new generation of faithful collectors. Some might argue that stimulating youth to collect coins is simply family fun, but the underlying dynamic reaches deep into our psyche: a rising generation of young numismatists strongly validates the collecting life. Of course, when one goes to sell a collection, it is always advantageous to have new collectors ready to buy.

An increasingly popular way to sell coins and gain recognition for one's collecting accomplishments is to consign your holdings to an auction. In this way, the collection is laid out for all to see, admire and covet. There are few compliments greater than to see others vying to possess your dearest specimens. In this context, auctions celebrate the collector. Competitive bidding provides direct feedback that is immediate and unadulterated. If the collection contains rarities, the collector's name might be associated with these lots. Even better, if the collection is comprehensive enough, the collector's name might appear in the subtitle of the auction announcement. This is the ultimate honor, as the collector is memorialized in the catalog, becoming part of the numismatic literature forever.

Auctions named for collectors are commonplace. It is like self-publishing. The practice has become part of numismatic culture. Each month brings forth a procession of collectors who have fulfilled the evanescent goal of completion. Headlines abound: "The John Ford collection revitalizes the colonial coin market," and "David Queller's collection ignites interest in the storied 1804 silver dollar." The media glorifies the sales; there is applause and smiling consignors, as prices realized break records. Glossy auction catalogs filled with photos become

The 1804 Draped Bust dollar is much more than a rare and exalted coin, it serves as a monument to immortalize past owners with a pedigree that reads Queller, Hawn, Lilliendahl, and Mickley. Such a coin protects you against obscurity and irrelevance.

epitaphs of a collecting life.

Auctions also insure that prized coins are dispersed to others who will value the coins highly. The exalted status of one's personal collection is secured. Fierce competition and high sale prices speak directly to the importance of the collection. Seeing others clamor for what you possess is an extremely rewarding experience, lending legitimacy to the collecting life.

It is important to remember that attached to each coin are memories that the

The 1804 Draped Bust dollar reverse.

collector has cherished. But upon disposal, he is all too aware that a new acquisition story is being written. A role in this new story matters, as many collectors want to be remembered as a former owner. Such thinking hints at animism, as a coin imbued with magic carries forward the spirits of all its owners.

The lineage of ownership has become a hot topic in the numismatic marketplace; particularly as improved media technology allows more accurate record keeping. The numismatic market routinely tracks the circulation of rare coins. Detailed pedigrees – once only known for the most illustrious coins – are readily available for lesser rarities. It is not unusual to find several auction slips attached to coins selling for just a few thousand (or even hundreds) of dollars. For sure, market valuation is one determinant of this tracking system. Yet, a pedigree entails a deeper significance; it declares that the coin is singular. It is the mark of a marvelous object! Few collectors are unaware of this noble attribute.

Pedigrees enhance the magical properties of coins by announcing membership into the numismatic elite while also marking the transience of ownership. To possess a coin once owned by a specialist suggests that the current collector, too, is a specialist. The mutual appreciation of the coin ties them together. Paradoxically, the lineage of ownership also relegates owners to the lesser status of temporary curators. Rather, the emphasis is placed on the "immortality" of the coin itself. As such, the permanence of the coin humbles all that owned it. The flights of fantasy that collectors so often indulge in when holding a historic coin is perhaps a direct expression of this awe. Pearce has observed in *Museums, Objects, and Collections*:

> *Objects ... have lives which, though finite, can be very much longer than our own. They alone have the power, in some sense, to carry the past into the present by virtue of their "real" relationship to past events ... . [An object] which carries meaning is able to do so because, unlike we ourselves who must die, it bears an "eternal" relationship to the receding past, and it is this that we experience as the power of "the actual object."*

Perhaps the most revered numismatic objects are the "trophy" coins. The Draped Bust silver dollar of 1804 and the 1913 Liberty nickel: these are the coins that are the most exalted. Their pedigrees represent a "who's who" in numismatics. Tradition has affixed names to these coins that are immortalized in the folktales of numismatics. For example, the Mickley specimen of the 1804 dollar (reportedly acquired from a Pennsylvanian bank in 1850) has become known by an ever-growing list of owners. In some cases only the most recent owner has been added (as in "the Queller-Mickley 1804 dollar"), but some catalogers have used a list derived from auction records (as in "the Queller-Hawn-Lilliendahl-Mickley 1804 dollar").

Lesser rarities still await names; for example the 1894 dimes are yet unnamed as are high-grade 1913-S quarters – immortality in the annals of numismatics awaits long-term owners of these and others. This tendency is reflected in Boka's *Provenance Gallery* wherein he provides biographical sketches of all the collectors who have owned the top 1794 large cents for each variety (Sheldon-17a to Sheldon-72). His work is both a tribute to the large cents themselves and a homage to those who loved them.

The pedigree becomes particularly significant at the time of disposal, as the collector yearns to be placed on the list. To be included alongside numismatic luminaries such as Louis Eliasberg, William Sheldon, and John Ford is no small measure. Yet, it is entirely possible, as these collectors amassed large collections that have long since been dispersed.

Even pedestrian pedigrees are appealing: a brief mention in an auction lot description will provide satisfaction for the average collector who is selling. At the lowest level, the details of a distant acquisition scribbled on a 2x2 manila envelope that goes with the coin will suffice. There are few greater honors than to be immortalized in the annals of numismatics, even if it is but a footnote. Here again, it is important to remember that disposal of a collection marks the endpoint of a life spent, and often organized around, collecting. We want others to remember this.

Numismatic culture has evolved to provide refuge from the fear that one's collecting is forgettable or meaningless. After all, this is where the anxiety lies at the end of the day. *Who else will appreciate what I have done?* A trip to any large convention provides the best medicine for these existential concerns. Here, the collector will find ample evidence to validate the whole enterprise of collecting.

Young collectors are gathered around the beginner forums while scouts participate in merit badge clinics. Exhibits, painstakingly assembled, tell the story of devoted collectors spending the best years of their lives seeking out just the right coin to complete their sets. Lifetime achievement awards – named for numismatic heroes – are conveyed annually. And in every corner, numismatic lore is being passed on. A subscription to a few periodicals allows the armchair and Internet-only collectors to experience it all vicariously. This gala perpetuates the illusion that everyone collects coins – it is the way of the world!

Indeed, the collecting process itself is a grand enterprise designed to create meaning in world full of chaos. No wonder that the end of collecting can ignite such anxiety. In this regard, Mieke Bal has suggested that the process of collecting represents "a gesture of endless deferral of death." The collector extends the collection, one piece at a time, thereby revitalizing the whole enterprise. The collection can end at any time, but each new acquisition makes it alive again. The collector controls this process and thereby controls life.

In a similar vein, Jean Baudrillard suggests in *The System of Collecting* that collecting provides power over a symbolic world (comprised of objects) that allows the collector to transcend the fear of death in order to feel safe from an unpredictable world. His view, however, eschews the role of collecting as immortality striving:

> *We should dismiss the cliché that man survives through his possessions. Creating a safe haven has really nothing to do with securing immortality ... but is a far more complex game which involves the 'recycling' of birth and death within an object system. What man wants from objects is not the assurance that he can somehow outlive himself, but the sense that from now on he can live out his life uninterruptedly and in a cyclical mode, and thereby symbolically transcend the realities of an existence.*

These interpretations borrow heavily from Sigmund Freud's ideas about coping with unconscious conflicts. The critical aspect is the notion that individuals must become immersed in the meaning systems of the collecting culture to avoid the salience of mortality. We are reminded by Freud's comment that "a collection to which there are no new additions is really dead" – according to Forrester in *Freud and Collecting*, Freud had stopped adding to his collection when he made this statement; he died a few months afterward.

I was sitting one evening, shortly after ... a hectic funeral week, surrounded by my books, thinking of them as a unique reflection of me. No one else in the world would put together quite this particular collection, which like me will be frozen in time, for just an instant, when I am gone, and then dispersed to hundreds of new owners. At least, that's the way I want it to be. I'm not a believer in institutional libraries. They lack the factor of loving care, which only a collector can bestow. The coin collections we build are equally unique – and evanescent. We build them like an image of ourselves. ...

— *Harry E. Salyards, Editor,* Penny-Wise, 1997

"At some level, we are likely to be awed, and enthralled, by the secret lives of our coins."

Getting Started: To Touch or Not to Touch

We touch everything we love. This is how we have experienced the world since birth. Collectors love their coins and want to touch them too. How else can we really connect with them, to embrace the magic of a timeworn cent or an unlikely Mint State survivor from yesteryear?

Our fingertips are endowed with millions of nerve endings. They represent the center of tactility – a big brain area is devoted to them. Consequently, our fingers are experienced, as we have put them just about everywhere! But herein lies the *rub*, our fingers are oily and dirty. Sure, we wash them with a thick, scented bar before handling our coins, but oil and dirt remain in enough quantities to do damage. Still we touch our coins: we cannot stop.

This is why museums rope off and incase their exhibits behind thick glass. Visitors are corralled along painted lines. No one is permitted to stray. Otherwise, some well-intentioned rogue will touch something, sit on something, or press against something; and this something will break! Can you imagine what would happen if the Smithsonian Museum left its unique 1849 $20 Double Eagle out on a podium to be caressed? Sooner or later, someone will get ice cream or chocolate on it! We all want to touch, but in a museum, we cannot.

Like a temple, the museum is operated with strict rules and decorum. Patrons whisper as not to interrupt others from pondering the collections there. An unwritten code of conduct allows wonderment and exclamation but requires a solemn and respectful demeanor. Only a few uniformed staff are permitted to step over the thickly woven ropes or enter the glass chambers. All this is designed to protect the objects from inquiring fingers.

This is why museums will never satisfy a collector. We want to be able to touch our coins – that is why we collect. This is how I commune with my Chain cent! Indeed, our frustration at being cordoned off from the enticing objects in a museum is assuaged by holding a significant coin in one's own hands. We all understand that coins provide a direct link to the past. Like *Coke: Original Formula*, coins are the "real thing!" They are pieces of history. We want to touch them because we want to experience the past – directly – in a way that history books, no matter how astutely written, simply fall short.

Paradoxically, the significance that we attribute to our coins demands that we mimic the curatorial standards that we see in museums. As with all prized objects, we tend to develop a set of rituals for handling our coins. The rules of engagement range from holding coins by their edges, to wearing gloves, to encapsulation in tamper-proof holders. The numismatic literature promulgates these preservation rituals, as it implores us to be "good numismatists."

Yet this level of restraint is not easy for many of us. I have succumbed to the urge often enough despite the *Angel of Numismatic Correctness* on my shoulder telling me that I was violating the curatorial rules of handling historic objects. "Shame on you for pressing your oily thumb into Ms. Liberty's face," the voice shouts. Next thing you know, I will be chastised for petting the Buffaloes!

There are three factors that shape our decision to "touch" or "not touch" our beloved coins. The first factor stems from the mystique that we attribute to the coin itself. At some level, we are likely to be awed, and enthralled, by the secret lives of

Oily and dirty fingers represent the greatest hazard for coins.

our coins. We hold them as truly sacred objects that bring the past into the present. Hence, we attribute a power to them that involves approach and avoidance tendencies. Simply put, we want to touch, but we know that the coin is special and must be protected from this urge. This power transforms the collector into a custodian whose goal is to preserve the object for posterity.

The second factor is more mundane and relates to our social identity as numismatists. We adhere to the rules of coin handling and preservation because we see ourselves as part of the collecting fraternity. We are indoctrinated to these rules on a regular basis by our exposure to magazines, books, and other collectors. Consequently, holding a coin by its edges is not only good curatorial practice, but also good etiquette. We internalize our coin handling skills just as we mind our manners.

The third factor is profane, yet in a market-driven collecting environment, is the most talked about. Here we are talking about the monetary value of our coins and the risks of personal loss that accompanies a coin with fingerprints, wear, or scratches that stem from mishandling. All the talk about third party graders returning coins as "Genuine (not gradable)" strike fear into collectors who have spent big bucks to obtain their coins. Even investors, who by definition could not care less about history, are prompted to adhere to strict curatorial rules when handling coins.

These factors shape how we balance the demand to protect our coins with the desire to enjoy them. On the one side, the risks stemming from oily fingertips and environmental effects such as moisture and dust particles are considered. On the opposite side, the availability of the coins to be viewed and studied is considered. There are trade offs to be evaluated, but fortunately, today's collector has many options that go well beyond the coin folder.

Since fingertips represent the biggest threat, we start by considering some of the holders that are available. The best holders on the market are the tamper-proof slabs used by professional grading companies. The newest versions hold the coin tightly and cannot be easily pried open by unruly fingers. I have passed slabs around the dinner table and dropped them on the floor without great concern; however, they are not soup proof, so it is best to wait until the actual eating is over. Hence, a reliable feature of slabs is their durability in the face of physical assault.

Many collectors bemoan slabs because they restrict access to the coins for study or the need to touch (precisely the point!). Nonetheless, the desire to study coins by photographing, weighing, or measuring them in some other way is legitimate in some cases. In my experience, many collectors just want to handle them in a ritualistic fashion in order to demonstrate to themselves (and to the *Angel*) how skilled they are. Indeed, ritualistic handling is very rewarding and reflects our power over the objects. Sometimes a slab can interfere with our rituals, as we cannot open the holder without breaking it apart.

One solution, that preserves the sturdiness of the slab, is to place coins in hard plastic holders that can be opened at will. There are several of these made of inert materials like acrylic and polyethylene that can be purchased from collecting supply stores. The coin fits tightly within or is bedded down with a rubberized ring to keep it snug. Like slabs, these containers will tolerate a short fall when dropped, but they are not water, or even, moisture proof – no holder is!

The pliant plastic coin envelope also allows ready access; this holder is known as the "flip" since it folds in half and is flipped open to insert a coin. A label can be inserted on the opposite side to record information about the coin. The flip allows the collector to take the coin in and out, but be aware that a certain amount of friction will occur during this exercise. For circulated coins, this might be quite satisfactory, but Mint State coins will suffer small scratches or "hairlines."

The plastic flip protects against fingertips only if the coin is left alone. However, we often cannot resist taking it out for a closer view, as the flip is deceptively easy to fold open. What we discover is that it is difficult to remove

the coin without pinching it on the rim with meaty fingers to pull it out – once again, the *Angel* will scowl at you. In addition, a pinched coin is hard to hold onto, particularly if the rim is worn smooth. I find it embarrassing to chase a rolling coin under the table in front of other collectors! Afterward, all talk is likely to center on whether or not the fall caused a rim bump while the red-faced collector tries to minimize the whole event: "Don't worry, it's a tough old coin!"

Plastic flips have another inherent hazard that must be watched for: namely, some types of plastic cause corrosion by leeching chemicals into the air. Flips made from polyvinylchloride (PVC) can impart a slimy green coating on a coin after a few months, the result of a chemical reaction that produces hydrochloric acid. It would be better to let the coin sit on a windowsill unprotected. The "unstable" flips tend to be soft and pliable which is too bad, as they are durable and comfortable to use.

In contrast, safer flips – made of Mylar – are brittle and sharp along the edges. These flips need to be replaced more often due to splitting, or else you will be chasing rolling coins with rim bumps. For this reason, many dealers and auction houses use the PVC flips for the short duration that they expect the coin to be in stock so that potential buyers can finger them without the plastic splitting at the seams. Once the coin is yours however, be sure to replace the flip with a Mylar one as soon as you can.

A cheaper version of the flip is the small coin envelope made out of sulfur-free paper. Of course, the flexibility to take the coin in and out is there, but not much else. You cannot see the coin, and the envelope provides no drop protection. Yet, some collectors enjoy the momentary feeling of anticipation that comes with gently sliding a coin out of its opaque envelope. In addition, envelopes can be written on, allowing ample space for cataloging important details about the coin that resides within.

Collectors of early American copper coins often use cotton inserts in their envelopes; this protects the reactive surfaces of copper from chemicals in the paper (mainly sulfides) and offers some modicum of drop protection. For these traditionalists, paper envelopes reflect a certain nostalgia for the "golden era" of collecting when plastics were not yet marketed; furthermore, some collectors muse that a large cent is more at home in a tattered paper envelope with scribbling on it, like the ones William Sheldon might have used.

Among the traditional holders are the many kinds of coin boards and coin folders that have been produced since the late 1930s. As discussed in previous chapters, the venerable coin folder has much to recommend it for circulated coins. The coins usually fit tightly in the holder (but make sure of this) and are protected by closing the folder. Of course, the reverse cannot be viewed when coins are placed in the simple cardboard folders, but bounded bookshelf albums with sliding Mylar windows do allow a full view. But again, be forewarned that sliding windows can impart hairlines to coins that are not seated deeply enough in these bookshelf albums.

Unlike slabs, flips, and envelopes, the folders allow a whole collection to be seen at a glance. This feature is wonderful for exhibiting your collection to others, as the broad array of coins is likely to impress even half-interested, but polite, viewers. For the collector and viewer alike, the folder defines the boundaries of the collection. In contrast, individual coin holders must be kept in a box and exhibited one by one.

There is one final holder option that is the most popular of all, but I hesitate to recommend it. This is the cardboard 2x2 with Mylar windows that is folded close and stapled on three sides. Yes, stapled – and that is the problem. Sooner or later, the collector is likely to scratch a coin on one of the staples when removing it. Why are they removing it? Because that is what collectors do! Sometimes an errant staple can scratch a coin that is contained in another holder when placed in a storage box together – so be sure to push all staples tightly close after stapling.

A staple imparts a thin but pronounced scratch on any coin it comes in contact with. The scratch will never go away! It takes a deft hand to slip the coin out of a cardboard 2x2 without catching at least the rim on a staple. Conscientious – and patient – collectors remove the staples completely before attempting to remove the coin, but as they decide what to do with the loose staples, the coin is often dropped, and we are back to chasing it.

As this thumbnail sketch shows (reminder: nails are part of the fingertips), the range of available holders is only as good as the collector's fine motor coordination with the exception of the lock-tight slab. Here again, the primary risk factors stem from the collector's own desire to touch, handle, study, and otherwise exercise their providence – however misguided – over their coins. Even slabs cannot withstand inquiring fingertips that have gained access to a small hacksaw!

Fingertips notwithstanding, environmental hazards are many. Fortunately, the chemistry of corrosion is well known; yet, it is hard to predict how an individual coin will react within a particular environment, as most hazards are invisible.

Extracting a Wheat Ear cent from a 2x2 holder is not easy. Fingertips and staples will smudge and scratch a coin – like this guy – if you are not careful!

Hence, it is a good strategy to attempt to mitigate all threats that moisture and pollutants can bring to a coin's surface. Ron Guth, author of *Coin Collecting for Dummies* and Scott Travers, author of *The Coin Collector's Survival Manual*, provide detailed discussions about preservation strategies that are enough to scare even casual collectors into purchasing cotton gloves and facemasks.

Everyone agrees that moisture is by far the worst culprit, as wet surfaces facilitate the kinds of chemical reactions that we want to avoid. Of course, coins need to be stored in a cool, dry place. In addition, the use of a silica gel, or other desiccant product, can absorb moisture from the air to keep a storage container dry. But more immediately, you should never spit on your coins – keeping in mind that breathing and talking while hovering over your coins is a surefire way to wet them with corrosive saliva!

Next on the list of chemical culprits are airborne sulfides (or compounds containing sulfur). These compounds are produced naturally by nature but are enhanced by burning fossil fuels. In short, these substances are everywhere! However, if a coin is placed in a relatively airtight container, then the surfaces of the coin will react to the sulfides within the holder only with no further damage after that. This is the best we can hope for. Nonetheless, several products are available that either coats the surfaces of holders to act as a shield against incoming air or that release a chemical that reduces the reactivity of metals to sulfides.

Finally, there are many particles that can instigate a chemical reaction; for example, rotting organic matter can produce sulfides. This is particularly obvious on coins dug from the ground. As before, moisture is always a co-conspirator in such cases. Less dramatic cases include small bits of paper from frayed coin envelopes or folders that contain minute amounts of sulfur. Remember also that these same holders soak up the oily debris from our fingertips. Certainly, it is a murky world out there, particularly at the microscopic level!

The chemical reaction that we want to avoid by keeping coins dry and away from sulfides is known as *oxidization*; this simply means that oxygen combines with other elements to produce corrosive changes in metals. We can see the corrosive process, as one that reduces the brilliance of freshly minted coins. When the colors produced are pleasing, collectors use terms such as "patina" or "toning" to describe the outcome. If the colors are blotchy or too dark, we call it "tarnish" or "corrosion." Either way, the surface of the coin is ever changing, as Scott Travers noted in the *Coin Collector's Survival Manual*: "No matter how beautiful any toning may be, it does represent an intermediate stage in the coin's progression to full darkening."

Copper, by far, is the most reactive of coinage metals. Typically, copper coins are orange and flashy at the time of minting, but with exposure to the elements described above, the coin shows a tendency to change colors like autumn leaves. Usually, old cents turn brown with oxidation, but red and yellow colors are not uncommon as the metal darkens. In advanced stages, small specks of carbon can form where the corrosion is concentrated; also, the surface can become porous and pitted as the metal is eaten away.

Many United States coins have copper in the mix; for example, nickels are 75 percent copper, whereas 10 percent of silver and gold coins are composed of copper alloy. Consequently, the reactivity of copper impacts other denominations to a lesser degree. Silver and gold tend to be less susceptible to developing porous surfaces, but carbon spots can develop on silver coins and blotches of copper toning are commonly found on gold coins. For the worried collector, prevention is the best medicine: that is, protection from the elements, and from fingertips.

A note on cleaning coins is needed here, as many collectors are tempted to try and remove carbon spots and blotchy toning. Most experts are clear on this: *Do not do it.* As mentioned earlier, cleaned coins are considered not gradable and are avoided like the plague. The risk of damage is just too great, as Ron Guth noted: "… the wood fibers in paper towels can actually scratch the surfaces of a coin." Nonabrasive methods of cleaning using solvents are more acceptable, but you need to learn how to do it. It is a precise skill that cannot be learned in a day. Professional conservation services are available for coins that suffer from PVC damage, dirt, and spotting.

Once the coins are protected, a final consideration regarding the security of the collection from thieves needs to be addressed. One strategy that many collectors employ is to keep the collection in a safety deposit box – but choose carefully, as some boxes are hot and damp. Hobby insurance is recommended even if you have selected a bank box that is secure. But remember that a typical policy will not cover damages due to a toxic storage environment.

In order to gain access to a collection, a few coins can be rotated out of the bank to enjoy at home. A hidden fireproof safe can be bolted to a cement floor or a major joist to protect the ones you have chosen to take out. This arrangement balances flexibility with peace of mind. Of course, there are risks associated with transporting coins to and from the bank. Collectors are encouraged to have a close friend or spouse accompany them while always keeping a watchful eye. Also, do not leave the coins in the car while you grab a sandwich: this is an all-to-common scenario for highway robbery!

One strategy that I have used to enjoy my coins involves creating a computer scrapbook of my collection. Each coin is photographed and placed in a computer file so that I can view them at my leisure. Most digital cameras are foolproof (lucky for me!). The computer files can be enlarged to produce high-resolution images that show more of the coin than I could ever explore with my eyes alone. You can take all of this a step farther by inserting the photos into a simple word processing file that allows you to make captions and comments.

A photo archive or scrapbook can be viewed on a big screen while you sit and enjoy it like a movie. But I left out the best part: you can do all of this without all the risks that fingertips bring! Of course, I will need to touch a few of them before too long. But for now, I can nibble on some chips *and* study my coins!

"...soon enough, an

exploratory purchase

is made. ..."

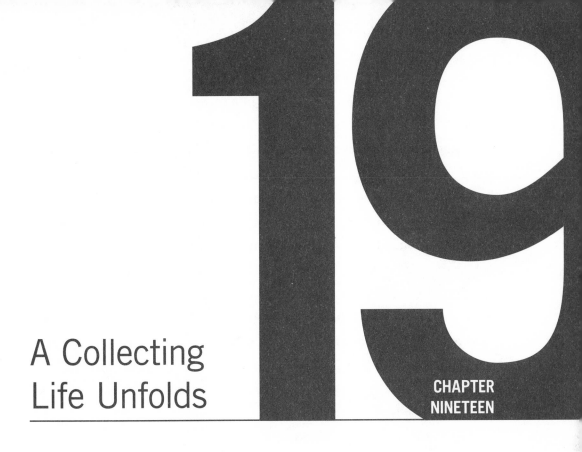

A Collecting
Life Unfolds

**CHAPTER
NINETEEN**

The script for a collecting life is often portrayed as wonderment narrowing toward specialization. V.E. Jenkins, writing in the June 1950 *The Numismatist*, captured this trajectory succinctly in three stages: the *Curiosity* stage, the *Learning* stage, and the *Knowing* stage. Initially, coins are discovered to be "delightful." The second stage culminates with the coin collector deciding which series to pursue. The final stage sharpens this focus, put bluntly by Jenkins, "the specialist … has his own field, and doesn't give a damn about the other series."

This linear progression has been promoted as the ideal collecting approach. It evolves toward an acquisition strategy that values taxonomic reasoning and set completion goals. Yet, Jenkins' three stages are more recommendation than reality, as his model is too simplistic and fails to capture the emotions and meanings that characterize collecting.

A cyclical model of collecting has been presented by McIntosh and Schmeichel, writing in the January-March 2004 issue of *Leisure Sciences*, that includes seven steps: 1) goal formation, 2) information gathering, 3) planning and courtship, 4) hunting, 5) acquisition, 6) post acquisition, and 7) cataloging and exhibiting. The strength of this model lies in the recognition that the collecting process is cyclic and driven by the intensifying emotions of courting and hunting – peaking at the moment of acquisition. This sequence represents the heart of the collecting experience.

One area where this model can be made more comprehensive involves the genesis and incubation of the collecting drive. It this regard, we are reminded that the collecting life often begins unannounced, as it is shaped by a mix of predisposing factors and often triggered by chance encounters with "interesting" coins – all this, before any awareness of "collecting" has pressed itself into consciousness. It is also important to include the end-stage of the collecting life, wherein the displacement of the collection is planned and the ultimate meaning of the collection is appraised.

This model is comprised of three broad stages of development: *Pre-Collecting, Active Collecting,* and *Post-Collecting.* Across stages, there are eight phases within the collecting life that play-out in a predictable order. Since collecting styles vary widely, the sequence of stages and phases provides a heuristic description of collecting dynamics – a master script if you will, from which actors routinely ad lib their lines, but rarely deviate far from the storyboard. The sometimes messy reality of classifying coin collectors was noted by an observer in the January 1943 *The Numismatist*:

> *Select any 10 coin collectors at random and you will find that each person had a different reason for starting the hobby. One became interested when a few old coins were given to him; another was intrigued by a few obsolete coins he had never seen before; another read a juicy advertisement on how to make a fortune in coins; another felt it would help occupy his mind, and still another really sensed the investment possibilities afforded. Scramble them all together and you have a composite of Mr. Average Collector.*

Whereas individual collecting narratives differ in the details, certain underlying determinants are shared, such as the pull of curiosity, the internalization of shared numismatic values, and the cycle of tension and release that underlies active collecting.

In the *Pre-Collecting Stage*, three phases occur: first, a predisposition to collect is nurtured; second, curiosity and interest are aroused; and third, awareness of an emerging collecting script unfolds. At the end of the third phase, a decision is made to consciously collect, or alternatively, to dismiss the notion. In the *Active Collecting Stage*, a four-phase process repeats itself. The fourth phase involves a courtship period that is governed by infatuation accompanied by a quest for information, and perhaps an impulsive or exploratory purchase, culminating in a selection of a specific collecting interest. Next comes hunting in phase five, wherein interest narrows considerably and specific search strategies are developed and tested. Acquisition follows the successful hunt; this phase is about triumph – it is the briefest of phases, sometimes passing in an instant. Phase seven begins with integrating the new acquisition into the collection. The excitement gives way to possession rituals that may be as brief as a journal notation or prolonged over weeks when the coin is examined and re-examined. The *Active Collecting Stage* comes full circle as integration gives way to a second courtship and hunt for the next coin.

At any time the cycle can slow – either due to collector fatigue or other extraneous factors (such as ageing, poor health or a poor economy) that lead to fading interest and enjoyment. At the same time, a second collecting interest can develop through phases two and three such that a second or third coin series emerges as the focus of a new infatuation in phase four. It is not unusual for collectors to experience several phases at once. For example, a collector can be scouring the bourse for a 1793 Chain cent while also taking a second look at New Jersey "horse and plow" coppers just to get a feel for them – hunting and courting at once!

If interest begins to fade and new prospects fail to excite, then the collector may enter the last phase, and a decision to stop collecting is made. Eventually, the collection is disposed of. The magic given to the coins may diminish at this point, but the memories and numismatic camaraderie often continue.

Phase One: Predisposition to Collect. We have seen that a broad, and

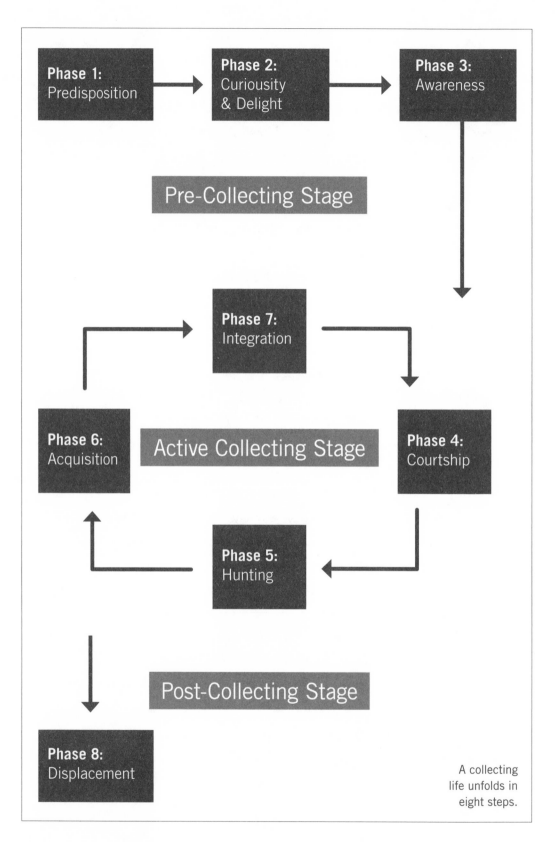

Phase 1: Predisposition

Phase 2: Curiousity & Delight

Phase 3: Awareness

Pre-Collecting Stage

Phase 7: Integration

Phase 6: Acquisition

Active Collecting Stage

Phase 4: Courtship

Phase 5: Hunting

Post-Collecting Stage

Phase 8: Displacement

A collecting life unfolds in eight steps.

unbridled, tendency toward collectivism is buried deep in the subcortical brain, a vestige of our hunter-gatherer ancestry. Developmental events conspire to shape this tendency into action. A drive to assemble, organize and classify is likely to motivate collecting for the sheer challenge of exercising these skills. The strength of this predilection may reflect the workings of a particularly sharp intellect coupled with an inquisitive nature. Perhaps coping with loss and uncertainty leads to the discovery that objects, by virtue of being available and loaded with sentimental value, can elicit feelings of security and well-being.

We are also reminded that, in children, this phase begets a period of "big pockets" collecting, as most youngsters pass through a developmental period wherein collecting is part of play. From turtles to rocks to coins – children amass whatever objects catch their fancy. This tendency peaks around 12 years of age, signaling when the brain boasts its highest level of neural interconnectivity. Sometimes collecting goes dormant as adolescence approaches, only to reappear later. The defining aspect of this phase is that collecting behaviors are emerging, for a variety of reasons, in children and adults, as a way of interacting with the world.

Phase Two: Curiosity and Delight. Labeled just as Jenkins suggested, this phase is defined by the arousal of deeply rooted impulses that move us toward novelty and complexity. Serendipitous coin finds arouse curiosity, but a specific desire to collect coins is not yet present. For example, a gift of a 2000-S Virginia silver proof quarter stimulates interest such that the person is intrigued enough to take a second look or even read about the *50 State quarters program*. There may be an accumulation of a few more quarters, as the budding collector notices another one in change and keeps it to compare to the proof specimen at home. These events might continue – New Mexico, Colorado, Arizona – but no conscious connection is made between these events.

These are critical events that will be recalled later as episodes that "sparked" an interest in collecting; yet, we see that this tendency has been simmering all along. Consequently, the defining aspect of this phase is a burgeoning interest that has focused collecting toward a preference for coins. The "accidental" collector tends to notice – even picks out from pocket change – State quarters, but he is not yet guided by a conscious decision to collect with a goal. Consequently, he does not search for what is missing, as he does not consider what he has already set aside. He is on the cusp of becoming a coin collector.

Phase Three: Awareness of a Collecting Interest. Over time these pre-collecting events begin to converge in awareness until the potential collector recognizes that he has developed a specific interest in State quarters – in fact, he has already been *accumulating* them. Many observers have labeled accumulation as an embryonic step that precedes collecting; but the defining characteristic *here* is the clear acknowledgment of interest. In an instant, the potential collector becomes aware of a series of events – seminal scenes – that define a collecting script.

It is at this point that specific events are remembered as the start of collecting. In fact, many coin collectors believe that one scene started it all, when actually, there were many events leading up to this day of reckoning. For example, the potential collector might have noticed an advertisement on television for State quarter proof sets; in that moment, he contemplates the idea of assembling a set of them – *this is the event he remembers.* He was primed to want them over the past few months, but now he has declared his interest and acknowledges a desire to collect them all. As Mieke Bal described, "Collecting comes to mean collecting precisely when a series of haphazard purchases or gifts suddenly become a meaningful sequence … that is the moment when a self-conscious narrator begins to 'tell' its story."

Along with his newfound awareness, a series of cognitive machinations occurs, as the neophyte collector questions the motives of his desire to collect State quarters: Is it history? Or geography? Is it investment? Or could it be driven by aesthetic considerations? No matter what, the quarters begin to reflect something important and personal. He is not sure of what it is exactly, but he finds himself musing about these coins and what they mean. A conscious decision to collect moves him to the fourth phase, transitioning from the *Pre-Collecting Stage* to the *Active Collecting Stage.*

Phase Four: Courtship. Infatuation is the dominant theme in this phase. Positive curiosity takes over, as tidbits of information are sought out and enjoyed for their ability to excite. This is the "liking" step where fantasy is allowed to override rational thinking. Collecting is not typically rule-governed at this juncture, as the collector is motivated by the thrill of exploration. Consequently, the collector may make some impulsive moves, such as acquiring a few coins to experience what possessing them feels like. The collector has not yet examined a particular series in enough detail to determine what collecting goals are realistic or even what goals promise the most enjoyment. Alternatively, some collectors may decide to follow the sage advice of reading the book before buying any coins – but soon enough, an exploratory purchase is made.

As the courtship process unfolds, the collector continues to explore reasons why particular coins "reach out and speak to him." The coins start to become imbued with significance that goes beyond history and art; rather, they become uniquely symbolic to the collector. Herein lies a crucial development: a deeper meaning is coalescing within. *Coins are becoming marvelous!*

On the surface, a coherent reason for collecting is being crafted; this explanation is likely to include both rationalizations (e.g., "They may be valuable one day.") and personal feelings (e.g., "I find these coins beautiful and soothing to look at."). At this juncture, the collector begins to look outwardly to the numismatic media for guidance and support. The chief outcome of the courtship phase is the adoption, even if cursory at first, of an identity of a collector with a specific interest or specialty coupled with a rationale for collecting. For example, "I am a collector of silver proof State quarters because I enjoy learning about the states!"

Phase Five: Hunting. Mobilization of resources directed toward searching for "special" coins characterizes the hunt. Coin-related research conducted at this point is more focused and specific to developing an acquisition plan: market pricing and availability are investigated. Curiosity is shaped by a *need to know* imperative, as the nuances of supply and demand are explored. Now that time and money is involved, reliable information is desperately wanted. At this point, widely diverse hunting styles become apparent. For example, the urgency of the hunt takes over for some, eroding rationality while fueling impulsive buys. On the other hand, some collectors adopt a more rational, even cautious, stance wherein a problem-solving approach is used to balance budget with desire. It is in the *thick of the hunt*, when collecting behaviors are the most visible, that we observe the full gamut of emotions and actions that characterize coin collectors.

Of course, collectors are always in the hunting mode, like hounds keenly sensitive to the smell of opportunity! The hunt is often considered the most enjoyable part of the hobby: confronting challenges while employing the totality of one's skills. We have seen that these are the elements of *flow* – peak experiences! The hunt is the most intense phase of collecting.

Phase Six: Acquisition. The moment of acquisition is climactic. The cascade of emotions is proportionate to the energy spent in courtship and in hunting. During auctions, winning the lot is celebrated like a victory in competitive sports. Adrenalin jolts the entire body. Many collectors relive the rush of acquisition over and over again, as they examine and re-examine their newly acquired coin.

With such emotional intensity, it is not surprising that collectors begin to wonder if their behavior is irrational. Incredulous spectators who question the time and energy committed, or the cash paid out, to acquire coins, begin to ask: Why? In response, collectors tend to seek out others to gain support, and validate their willingness to go to such lengths to obtain the "right" coin.

Phase Seven: Integration. The integration phase can vary widely across collectors. Some simply move ahead, planning for the next acquisition, whereas others take time to explore how the new acquisition compliments the collection. Many numismatic pundits have encouraged collectors to enjoy their coins by studying them and learning about their history. The *Integration Phase* reflects the acumen of the numismatist, as inclusion rituals mature. Cataloging and research might occur after each acquisition, or at intervals following several acquisitions. Preparing an exhibit or a lecture is also considered to reflect this process at its highest levels of sophistication. The hallmark of integration involves the contemplation of the significance (both personal and numismatic) of each coin – it is a celebration of possession.

Phases six and seven resolve in a return to the fourth phase. The *Courtship* phase is likely to go more quickly the next time around, as the collector has already spent considerable time outlining a specific acquisition strategy. In addition, the cycle might overlap on itself, as the collector pursues several goals at once, as in collecting State quarters and beginning date by mint sets of Lincoln cents and Jefferson nickels. In addition, some exploratory purchases of silver quarters might be made – hence, planning and research start anew in contemplation of starting a collection of silver Washington quarters.

Phase Eight: End of Collecting and Displacement. There comes a time when the collection is placed in storage without further acquisitions or is bequeathed, donated, or sold. As the zest for hunting and acquisition fades, concerns about preserving the collection or dispersing its contents to other devoted collectors become paramount. After all, the collection represents the culmination of a life's work. All collectors want others to appreciate what has been accomplished. Hence, the *Displacement Phase* of the collecting life is momentous. That one or two outstanding specimens can be placed in the hands of another who will cherish them is often reward enough for most collectors.

The *Collecting Life* reflects a microcosm of all that is unique about humanity. We are meaning-makers, striving to create enduring stories that make sense of our world, while also – as creators and curators – affording us a supporting role. Coin collecting is a narrative of our life spelled out with objects. Coins are marvelous because we appreciate the stories that came before, just as we write new ones for those who will come later.

"This is a noble pursuit.

The collector is a

passionate hunter."

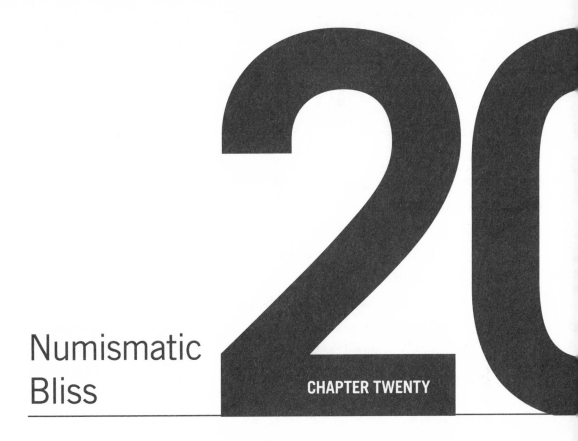

Numismatic Bliss

CHAPTER TWENTY

How does one achieve numismatic bliss? One sage, whose identity is now lost to the ages, offered: "Happiness is a complete set of Morgan dollars." Another wise man said, "Happiness is a complete set of Lincoln cents." Few coin collectors will disagree. So, how does completing a collection bring happiness?

We are reminded that the act of collecting coins transforms them into marvelous objects. No longer pocket change, coins become singular objects that require special care. Such coins transcend ordinary experience. For the collector to have the opportunity to decide what role the coin will play in the collection is immensely gratifying. Here lies the enjoyment of coin collecting. *This is numismatic bliss!*

The essence of collecting is to *create* something significant. It is a process that unfolds as the collection grows and matures. Collecting reflects our deepest motives. It represents our maneuvering to control, order-up, and make sense of the world. We experience this as a passionate endeavor, but one with the utmost seriousness – precisely because it is of our own making. As philosopher Jean Baudrillard noted in *The System of Collecting*, "Although a collection may speak to other people, it is always first and foremost a discourse directed toward oneself." Indeed, as the last chapter made clear, a collection is a narrative: a story of *A Collecting Life*.

Specific reasons given for collecting rarely satisfy because they miss this big picture. Coin collectors will often say: "I am addicted," or "I love history," or "I have a talent for organizing and classifying things," and so on. But these are only bits of the collecting life – tips of an iceberg. A closer, more comprehensive, look reveals that much more is at stake. At its core, collecting – coins or Dixie cup lids – represents our will toward self-determination. *Caught in the Act of Collecting*, as Marilynn Karp entitled her book, is all about collectors asserting themselves to create something meaningful.

This is collecting at its highest level. It is a life story that includes chapters on curiosity, challenge, flow, and friendships. And what great stories are being told! Every day great collections are being created while past collections are being dispersed. Many rarities are still being discovered. Attic caches, shipwrecks, die varieties, condition census coins – the hunt is on! Triumphs of cherry picking fueled by passion fill the annals of numismatics. These are exciting times!

The most enduring metaphor for coin collecting has been the thrill of the hunt. This is a noble pursuit. *The collector is a passionate hunter.* But this hunt is about creating something meaningful. It is all about self-expression. In this light, we can see how the metaphor of addiction seems out of place when describing the collecting life. Even love is not enough of an explanation. Similarly, we can appreciate how rationalizations about investment and "stores of value" only dilute the experience of collecting.

What conclusions can we draw from all of this? Is there a recipe that is uniquely informed by the psychology of collecting that can help collectors achieve numismatic bliss? Yes, there is. But the ingredients are not deep secrets buried in the psyche. In fact, most veteran coin collectors have long since discovered them. Five ingredients stand out as fundamental to the quest for numismatic bliss. They are labeled as follows: 1) Embracing the Urge to Collect, 2) Nurturing Curiosity, 3) Allowing Flexible Rules, 4) Setting Realistic Goals, and 5) Maintaining Balance.

Embracing the Urge to Collect. Collectors have become accustomed to on-lookers who raise their eyebrows and look askance at their game of solitaire – we know that they are dumbfounded despite their good intentions to appear curious and interested. Even collectors can be at a loss for words to explain. In this context, the first ingredient of numismatic bliss implores coin collectors to embrace their urge to collect and accept it as part of their being. It is not a biological aberration or addiction, yet collecting does have physiological aspects that harkens back to our ancestral roots. This urge is shaped by our experiences – good and bad – but it is no less commendable whether it reflects coping or capriciousness.

To the contrary, the acceptance of the urge to collect embraces our adaptive strengths in the guise of curiosity, openness to experience, and the exercise of cognitive abilities that allow us to discriminate between objects on all sorts of dimensions (by type, variety, condition, etc.). These are talents, like music and tinkering that can be nurtured or ignored. Choosing to collect represents an assertion of these talents. Thomas Elder, past ANA president, writing in the December 1916 issue of *The Numismatist* expressed this sentiment:

> *The best type of collector is a most valuable member of society. By the best collector I mean one whose pursuit, study and research in connection with his hobby have magnified his imaginative, esthetic, romantic and intellectual qualities. His wide and varied experiences with various odd and interesting objects, and his painstaking care of them, have given him a remarkable fund of out-of-the-way information, as well as patience, a sense of order and practicality. Contrary to current opinion, the best collector is far from eccentric. He is the finest sort of an example of the cultured and refined man.*

Such a glowing endorsement! Too often collectors neglect to recognize these qualities in themselves. Suffice to say, collecting adds a new dimension to life that can be extremely rewarding.

Nurturing Curiosity. All interests wax and wane throughout life; hence, collecting fatigue is likely to occur at times. Typically, a bout of fatigue ends when new opportunities are discovered, spurring the development of a second or third collecting enterprise. The second ingredient of numismatic bliss is to inject the elements of novelty and complexity into collecting on a regular basis such that fatigue rarely diminishes the wonderment that is an integral part of the allure. This involves an active, and deliberate, seeking out of new experiences such that the collector is exposed to fresh collecting fields on a regular basis. In this way, the hunt is prolonged indefinitely!

Reading numismatic periodicals and interacting with other hobbyists (including those who are pursuing different series) can provide a steady stream of coin adventures that stimulate curiosity. Indeed, it is an old adage that states: collectors who explore the wider history surrounding coins can make any folder of coins infinitely more appealing. As one collector quipped in the January 1958 issue of *The Numismatist*: "Your coins can help you to qualify for more $64,000 contests than any professor of, or classes in, history, mythology, geography, biography and a dozen other fields of learning."

Consequently, it behooves collectors to

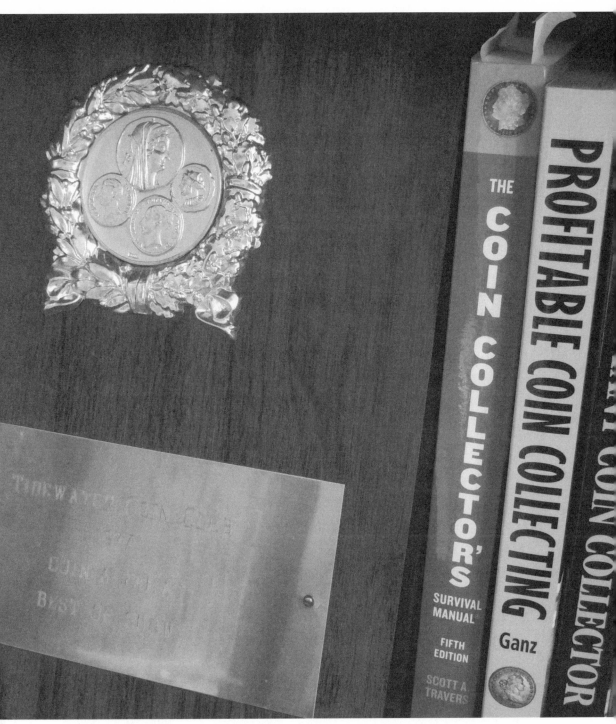

An award for Best in Show reflects the culmination of a life spent collecting – that glow you feel is *numismatic bliss*.

look beyond the parade of dates and mints and consider the secret lives of coins – how they were designed, minted, spent, and dispersed. This helps to imbue coins with greater significance. Q. David Bowers exemplifies this approach in his guidebooks, wherein he makes great effort to stimulate curiosity about how the coins were used in daily life; for instance, in this *Guidebook of Shield and Liberty Head Nickels*, he devotes several sections exploring nickelodeons, coin-operated music boxes, and carnival arcades. As he put it:

> *To me, a single nickel can offer a "program" of delights if contemplated …. In the early 20th century a nickel was the passport to many pleasures for young and old – the 5-cent cigar, the 5-cent glass of beer, a chance at hitting the jackpot in an ornate Caille-brand slot machine, and admission to a nickelodeon theater.*

Such images make the coins come alive! It may also prompt interests in exonumia that are likely to enhance the coin collecting life in unpredictable, but immensely satisfying, ways.

Allowing Flexible Rules. Coin collecting is a rule-governed activity shaped by curatorial traditions and implicit standards held dear by the numismatic fraternity. These rules apply to the care and feeding of coins as well as to the appropriate ways to collect – for example, set completion versus accumulation. At times, the mores of numismatic correctness can be stifling and distract from the sense of autonomy that is critical for any creative endeavor like coin collecting. The third ingredient of numismatic bliss encourages collectors to be flexible in choosing the manner in which one wishes to collect. Certainly, the traditions of the hobby reflect accumulated wisdom; yet, there is ample room for the individual to pursue his interests and experience coins in their own unique way.

In this regard, a flexible approach defined by one's temperament is essential to reap the greatest rewards from collecting. Set completion can be defined in many ways that go beyond date-by-mint collecting or type set collecting. One of the greatest joys of collecting is to define, and redefine, the boundaries of the collection as it grows. It is more important for the coins collected to reflect the true interests of the collector, rather than some external standard that defines what must be included or what condition grade represents the "smart" choice. David Harper, editor of *Numismatic News*, candidly expressed the importance of flexibility as follows (Sept. 9, 2009):

> *… one of the reasons I became a coin collector is I could do anything I wanted that appealed to me. I made mistakes. I bought some silly things along the way, but I was doing what I wanted to do – I wasn't doing something good for me (at least I didn't realize that I was). Trying to take the spontaneity out of collecting is a surefire way to kill it.*

Too often, collectors become disenchanted with set completion goals due to high prices, fading interest, or competing desires; yet, they persevere like accidental marathoners who got caught in the rush. Alternatively, some collectors may be the happiest when they allow themselves to "dabble" in diverse areas of numismatics, thereby stimulating curiosity while also broadening their collecting sphere. Edward Rochette, numismatic researcher and journalist, shared his flexible collecting focus as follows: "I care not for condition, I seldom complete a series, my collection is more of an accumulation than the orderly quest of acquisition, but I enjoy my collection as one would a good book."

Setting Realistic Goals. When coin collecting went mainstream in the 1930s following the introduction of the coin board, setting goals was simple: everything was laid out in front of you with each coin in the series having its own labeled hole. But these times have largely passed, as today's collector is confronted with a vast collecting field. Thanks to a robust numismatic media, collectors can purchase just about anything, on any given day, over the telephone or with the click of a computer mouse. Choices abound, and so do opinions about "smart" or "proper" collecting.

Consequently, many collectors have allowed their own collecting goals to be shaped, even usurped, by what is promoted in the numismatic press. In addition, many collectors are apt to measure their goal attainment progress by what others have accomplished. We know where this can lead, as defining one's collecting goals on established criteria (but not one's own) for completing sets often brings frustration. The fourth ingredient of numismatic bliss should be obvious in this case: collectors who set realistic goals, even those who must think outside the folder or guidebook in order to do so, are likely to enjoy collecting at a higher level.

A critical aspect of goal setting that can erode the enjoyment of collecting involves the pitfalls inherent with social comparison. Hence, a corollary of this guideline insists that the goal be of the collector's own choosing. Collecting in a mass-media environment where the efforts of other collectors are well publicized, may prompt some collectors to adversely judge themselves, feeling that their "meager" collection is inadequate, or worse, that their numismatic competence is lacking. In years past, before the age of Internet forums and daily auctions, a coin hobbyist could assemble some "nice looking" sets that would surely bring admiration at the local coin club or show. Nowadays, it is much more difficult to impress, as so many "better" collections are available to see. In short, the comparative field has grown so dramatically, that it is more difficult for the average collector to feel that they have accomplished something extraordinary.

This dynamic has been widely discussed among psychologists studying rates of happiness in modern society. One of the chief findings is that as the number of choices increase in the marketplace, the potential for regret – and the negative feelings that go with it – is greater. The comparative field is just too large to fully evaluate. Consequently, the numismatic maxim to buy only the best becomes overwhelming and has a tendency to cause more dread than satisfaction. How does one choose the best 1909-S VDB when 10 of them are on the market today, and another 10 will be available to consider in the next few months?

Consequently, it is important for collectors to set goals that reflect their own vision of what they want to create, and not to be lured into the demands of the marketplace that promotes high grade, high rarity, high salability coins! Red Henry, an early copper collector writing in the January 1995 issue of *Penny-Wise*, pointedly encouraged collectors to avoid the pitfalls of social comparison: "… don't let others write the rules for your game. Don't worry about other people's grades, goals, or standards – just find a coin you like to own, and stick with it."

We have seen that collecting is about meaning-making wherein enjoyment comes from the act of creating something that tells a story about history, art, or set completion. But of course, numismatic competence comes in many flavors including market savvy. Some collectors enjoy the competitive marketplace: they get the most satisfaction from *winning* the "best" coin. Nothing bad about that! From condition registries to copper *whist* matches, coin collecting can be a competitive sport. Either way – whether angling or appreciating – the same ingredients for numismatic bliss apply: reasonable goals that are tailored to one's own interests (and budget) represent a time-tested path to enjoyment.

Maintaining Balance. There is a thick literature on collecting obsessions that warn of over-exuberance coupled with the neglect of personal responsibility. But, it is not collecting *per se* that is the problem; rather, like all pleasurable desires, self-discipline is needed. It is important to pursue coins in a manner that does not interfere with the ability to care for oneself, make a living, and have satisfactory relationships. As with all desires in life, balance is important. The ingredient of balance rounds out the whole recipe for numismatic bliss, as it requires that collectors both accept the collecting urge as a positive behavioral trait, but also, that collectors assert control over their desires and not overdo it.

Collecting can, and does, adversely impact the collector and their family. For the collector, the most common problem entails the narrowing of focus such that collecting becomes the chief source of enjoyment in life. As Goldberg and Lewis describe in their book, *Money Madness: The Psychology of Saving, Spending, Loving, and Hating Money*:

> *Objects ultimately become more important than people, and fanatic collectors progressively alienate themselves from friends and family, occasionally even becoming suspicious that others will take away their prized possessions. They tend to withdraw from interpersonal relationships and often do not concern themselves with everyday problems like paying bills or getting the car serviced.*

The above description suggests that collecting can also adversely impact family members. As Russell Belk described in the *Journal of Economic Psychology*, "For all but the most affluent, the presence of a collector in the household means that money that might otherwise be spent on joint or individual consumption by other family members is spent on the collector and collection." Added to the cost of the coins themselves are the costs for hunting trips, storage, supplies, books, and the like … not to mention, the time involved in collecting activities.

Indeed, collecting is not wholly rational; passions often rule the day. In addition, we are reminded, once again, by Harry Rinker's observation that true collectors are never satisfied – they are always hunting. Ponder this: Can you identify an active collector who is not yearning for some rarity or upgrade? Probably not! Furthermore, collectors are always reaching for those coins that seem to be just out of reach! This is clearly evident at auctions where competitive bidding propels collectors to lofty – and unfortunately unaffordable – heights. Leslie Hindman, auctioneer and author of *Adventures at the Auction*, described the exuberance:

> *I can spot a victim of auction fever as far back as row 50. It is the person who has to be the first bidder on every lot he wants. He's the guy who thrusts his paddle into the air and waves it back and forth as if he's greeting a returning armada. He's the guy nervously pacing back and forth along the sidelines. He's the guy who avidly looks for every person who dares bid against him. He's the guy who buys everything at top dollar. And he's the guy most likely to approach me later begging me to cut him a deal because he has overpaid for everything and his wife is going to kill him when she finds out.*

If your spouse is going to kill you … enough said! Clearly, collecting costs everyone in the household, so it is important to be cognizant of the happiness of others.

On a more positive note, maintaining balance also keeps the collecting urge crisp and exciting. Few activities can be rewarding all the time. For many collectors, coin shows tend to be new and exciting when they happen only a few times per year. Each collector must discover his own threshold. Besides, there are many other ways to enjoy numismatics between hunts – whether it is reading and research or socializing with others who also find coins marvelous.

We come to a conclusion at this point, where this introspective journey ends. It is time to get back to our coins and to plan the next hunting expedition. We always knew coins were marvelous; and now we understand that it is collectors themselves who transform these diminutive bits of metal into something special. Our passion for coins reflects a yearning to assert our powers of self-expression.

We are fortunate to have found this passion. And we are better for it.

Bibliography

Allen, B. and Potter, K. *Strike It Rich with Pocket Change*. Iola, WI: Krause, 2006.

Anderson, S.W., Damasio, H. and Damasio, A.R. "A Neural Basis for Collecting Behaviour in Humans." *Brain* 128 (2004): 201-212.

Author. "The Mystery of Coins." *American Journal of Numismatics* 24 (Jul. 1889): 36.

-----. "Coin Collecting: A Stabilizing Influence." *The Numismatist* 56 (Apr. 1943): 280.

-----. "Numismatics and Numismatic Societies." *American Journal of Numismatics* 2 (Jun. 1867): 3-6.

-----. "Numismatics as a Hobby." *American Journal of Numismatics* 2 (Feb. 1867): 1.

Bal, Mieke. "Telling Objects: A Narrative Perspective on Collecting." *The Cultures of Collecting*. Eds. J. Elsner & R. Cardinal. London, UK: Reaktion, 1994. 96-115.

Balter, L. "Magic and the Aesthetic Illusion." *Journal of the American Psychoanalytic Association* 50 (2002): 1163-1195.

Baudrillard, Jean. "The System of Collecting." *The Cultures of Collecting*. Eds. J. Elsner & R. Cardinal. London, UK: Reaktion, 1994. 7-24.

Baumeister, R. F. and Leary, M. R. "The Need to Belong: Desire for Interpersonal Attachments as a Fundamental Human Motivation." *Psychological Bulletin* 117 (1995): 497-529.

Belk, Russell. "Collectors and Collecting." *Interpreting Objects and Collections*. Ed. Susan Pearce. New York: Routledge, 1994. 317-326.

-----. "Collecting as Luxury Consumption: Effects on Individuals and Households." *Journal of Economic Psychology* 16 (1995): 477-490.

-----. "The Ineluctable Mysteries of Possessions." *To Have Possessions: A Handbook on Ownership and Property*. Ed. F. W. Rudmin. *Journal of Social Behavior and Personality* 6 (1991): 17-55.

-----. *Collecting in a Consumer Society*. New York: Routledge, 1995.

Bell, C.H. "A Defense of Collectors." *American Journal of Numismatics* 2 (Oct. 1876): 39.

Berlyne, Daniel. "Novelty, Complexity, and Interestingness." *Studies in the New Experimental Aesthetics*. Ed. Daniel Berlyne. Washington DC: Hemisphere, 1974. 175-180.

-----. *Conflict, Arousal, and Curiosity*. New York: McGraw-Hill, 1960.

Boka, Jon. *Provenance Gallery of the Collectable Copper Cents Varieties of the United States Mint from the Year 1794*. San Ramon, CA: Falcon, 2005.

Bowers, Q. David. *The Expert's Guide to Collecting & Investing in Rare Coins*. Atlanta, GA: Whitman, 2005.

-----. *A Guide Book of Lincoln Cents*. Atlanta, GA: Whitman, 2008.

-----. *A Guide Book of Shield and Liberty Head Nickels*. Atlanta, GA: Whitman, 2006.

-----. *The History of United States Coinage as Illustrated by the Garrett Collection*. Wolfeboro, NH: Bowers and Merena Galleries, 1979.

Breen, Walter. *Walter Breen's Complete Encyclopedia of U.S. and Colonial Coins*. New York: F.C.I. Press and Doubleday, 1988.

-----. *Walter Breen's Encyclopedia of Early United States Cents: 1793-1814*. Wolfeboro, NH: Bowers and Merena Galleries, 2000.

Bressett, Kenneth. ed. *The Official American Numismatic Association Grading Standards for United States Coins*. 6th ed. Atlanta, GA: Whitman, 2006.

Brewer, M. B. and Gardner, W. "Who is this 'We'? Levels of Collective Identity and Self Representations." *Journal of Personality and Social Psychology* 71 (1996): 83-93.

Brown, M. and Dunn, J. *A Guide to the Grading of United States Coins.* Atlanta, GA: Whitman, 1962.

Burke, J. *The Gods of Freud: Sigmund Freud's Art Collection.* New York: Knopf & Random House, 2006.

Buss, D. M. "The Evolution of Happiness." *American Psychologist* 55 (2000): 15-23.

Bust Half Nut Club. www.busthalfprices.com/bhnc.php 27 Jan. 2008.

Csikszentmihalyi, M. *Finding Flow: The Psychology of Engagement with Everyday Life.* New York: HarperCollins, 1997.

-----. *Flow: The Psychology of Optimal Experience.* New York: HarperCollins, 1990.

Danet, Brenda and Katriel, Tamar. "No Two Alike: The Aesthetics of Collecting." *Interpreting Objects and Collections.* Ed. Susan Pearce. New York: Routledge, 1994. 220-239.

Deisher, Beth. "Activity in Moderns Real, Sustainable?" Coin World Online. Amos Press, 20 Jan. 2003. www.coinworld.com 11 Jan. 2008.

-----. *Making the Grade: A Grading Guide to the Top 25 Most Collected U.S. Coins.* Sidney, OH: Amos, 2005.

Dittmar, H. "Meanings of Material Possessions as Reflections of Identity: Gender and Social-material Position in Society. To Have Possessions: A Handbook on Ownership and Property. Ed. F. W. Rudmin. *Journal of Social Behavior and Personality* 6 (1991): 165-186.

Dolnick, M. "Discovering New Die 'Varieties.'" *The Numismatist* 74 (Jan. 1961): 9-10.

Early American Coppers Society. www.info@eacs.org

Elder, Thomas. "Collecting – With Special Reference to Coins, Medals and Paper Money." Dec. 1916. *Selections from the Numismatist: United States Coins.* Ed. American Numismatic Association. Atlantic, GA: Whitman, 1960. 37-50.

Engleman, E. "A Memoir in Bergasse 19: Sigmund Freud's Home and Offices, Vienna 1938." *Photographs of Edmund Engleman.* New York: Basic Books, 1976. 131-143.

Fisher, Helen. *Why We Love: The Nature and Chemistry of Romantic Love.* New York: Henry Holt, 2004.

Fivaz, Bill and Stanton, J.T. *The Cherrypickers' Guide to Rare Die Varieties of United States Coins: Volume II.* 4th ed. Atlanta, GA: Whitman, 2006.

Formanek, Ruth. "Why They Collect: Collectors Reveal their Motivations." *To Have Possessions: A Handbook on Ownership and Property.* Ed. F. W. Rudmin. *Journal of Social Behavior and Personality* 6 (1991): 275-286.

Forrester, J. (1994). "'Mille etre': Freud and Collecting." *The Cultures of Collecting.* Eds. J. Elsner & R. Cardinal. London, UK: Reaktion, 1994. 224-252.

Full Step Nickel Club. www.fullstepjeffersonnickels.com

Gans, E. "Reminiscences of an Old Collector." *The Numismatist* 77 (Oct. 1964): 1363-1365.

Giedd, J.N., Blumenthal, J., Jefferies, N.O., et. al. "Brain Development during Childhood and Adolescence: A Longitudinal MRI Study." *Nature and Neuroscience* 2 (1999): 861-863.

Gillilland, Cory. Quotation. Ed. Q. David Bowers. *The Numismatist's Downtown Companion, Volume 7.* Wolfeboro, NH: Bowers and Mercena, 1994. 13-14.

Goldberg, H. and Lewis, R. T. *Money Madness: The Psychology of Saving, Spending, Loving, and Hating Money.* New York: William Morrow, 1978.

Goldberg, Lewis. "The Development of Markers for the Big-Five Factor Structure." *Psychological Assessment* 4 (1992): 26-42.

Goldstein, R.Z. and Volkow, N.D. "Drug Addiction and Its Underlying Neurobiological Basis: Neuroimaging Evidence for the Involvement of the Frontal Cortex." *American Journal of Psychiatry* 159 (2002): 1642-1652.

Guth, Ron. *Coin Collecting for Dummies.* New York: Wiley, 2001.

Harper, David, ed. *North American Coins and Prices: 2011.* Iola, WI: Krause, 2010.

-----. "Class of 63: Free Choice Makes Collecting What It Is." *Numismatic News,* 9 Sep. 2008 www.numismaticnews.net 2 Jan. 2009.

Harry W. Bass Jr. Money Museum. www.money.org

Henry, R. "Marching to Your Own Drummer: A Comment on EAC Diversity." *Penny-Wise* (1995): 40.

Hindman, L. *Adventures at the Auction.* New York: Clarkson Potter, 2001.

Jenkins, V. E. "The Philosophy of Coin Collecting." *The Numismatist* 63 (Jun. 1950): 354.

Johnson, C. M. "U.S. Numismatic Literature." *The Numismatist* 76 (Jan. 1963): 23-32.

Johnston, Susan. *Collecting: The Passionate Pastime.* New York: Harper & Row, 1986. 13-15.

Kalivas, P.W. and Volkow, N.D. "The Neural Basis of Addiction: A Pathology of Motivation and Choice." *American Journal of Psychiatry* 162 (2005): 1403-1413.

Karp, Marilynn. *In Flagrante Collecto (Caught in the Act of Collecting).* New York: Abrams, 2006.

King, W.D. *Collections of Nothing.* Chicago: University of Chicago, 2008.

Lange, David. *Coin Collecting Boards of the 1930s & 1940s: A Complete History, Catalog and Value Guide.* Brandenton, FL: D. Lange, 2007.

Litman, J. A. "Curiosity and the Pleasures of Learning: Wanting and Liking New Information." *Cognition and Emotion* 19 (2005): 793-814.

Masson, J. M. *The Complete Letters of Sigmund Freud to Wilhelm Fliess, 1887-1904.* Cambridge, MA: Belknap, 1985.

McIntosh, W.D. and Schmechel, B. "Collectors and Collecting: A Social Psychological Perspective." *Leisure Sciences* 26 (2004): 85-97.

McNall, B. and D'Antonio, M. *Fun While it Lasted: My Rise and Fall in the Land of Fame and Fortune.* New York: Aureus Ventures, 2003.

Mills, B. "Coin Collecting as a Hobby and Investment." *The Numismatist* 56 (Jan. 1943): 11-13.

Montgomery, P., Borchardt, M., and Knight, R. *Million Dollar Nickels: Mysteries of the Illicit 1913 Liberty Nickels Revealed.* Irvine, CA: Zyrus Press, 2005.

Morin, V. "That Crazy Fad of Coin Collecting." *The Numismatist* 54 (Dec. 1941): 935-936.

Muensterberger, Werner. *Collecting: An Unruly Passion: Psychological Perspectives.* Princeton, NJ: Princeton University Press, 1994.

Mullin, B. & Hogg, M. A. "Motivations for Group Membership: The Role of Subjective Importance and Uncertainty Reduction. *Basic and Applied Social Psychology* 21 (1999): 91-102.

National Silver Dollar Roundtable. www.silverdollarroundtable.com 9 Jan. 2011.

Nawrocki, W.S. "Numismaticitis: A Non-fatal Social Disease." *The Numismatist* 94 (Aug. 1981): 2129-2131.

Newman Money Museum. www.newmanmoneymuseum.org

Observer. "Collecting Run Mad." *American Journal of Numismatics* 11.1 (Jan. 1877): 54-56.

Observer. "Is this Numismatics?" *The Numismatist* 53 (Jul. 1940): 492-493.

Overton, A. *United States Half Dollar Die Varieties: 1794-1836.* Third ed. Escondido, CA: Don Parsley, 1990.

Pearce, Susan. "Collecting Reconsidered." *Interpreting Objects and Collections.* Ed. Susan Pearce. New York: Routledge, 1994. 193-204.

-----. *Collecting in Contemporary Practice.* Walnut Creek, CA: Sage, 1998.

-----. *Museums, Objects, and Collections: A Cultural Study.* Washington, D.C.: Smithsonian Institution, 1992.

Pijewski, J. "Chapter 12: EDNA, or the Other Woman." *Penny-Wise* (Jan. 2003): 32-37.

Pipes, G. A. "The Collecting Instinct." *The Numismatist* 52 (Dec. 1939): 994-996.

-----. "As Others See Us." *The Numismatist* 59 (Jan. 1946): 32.

Reid, S. A. and Hogg, M. A. "Uncertainty Reduction, Self-enhancement, and Ingroup Identification." *Personality and Social Psychology Bulletin* 31 (2005): 804-817.

Reiter, Ed. *The New York Times Guide to Coin Collecting.* New York: New York Times, 2002.

Rigby, Douglas and Rigby, Elizabeth. *Lock, Stock, and Barrel: The Story of Collecting.* Philadelphia, PA: J.B. Lippincott, 1944.

Rinker, Harry. *How to Think Like a Collector.* Cincinnati, OH: Emmis, 2005.

Roberts, A.C. "The Numismatist's Dream." *American Journal of Numismatics* 4 (Mar. 1870): 81-83.

Rochette, Edward. Quotation. Ed. Q. David Bowers. *The Numismatist's Downtown Companion, Volume 7.* Wolfeboro, NH: Bowers and Mercena, 1994. 17.

Ruddy, James. *Photograde: Official Photographic Grading Guide for United States Coins.* Irvine, CA: Zyrus, 2005.

Ryan, R. M. & Deci, E. L. "Self-Determination Theory and the Facilitation of Intrinsic Motivation, Social Development, and Well-being." *American Psychologist* 55 (2000): 68-78.

Saeman, C. C. "To the New Collector." *The Numismatist* 74 (Nov. 1961): 1528-1529.

Salyards, H. E. Editorial. *Penny-Wise* (Mar. 1997).

-----. "Grading (Again)." Editorial. *Penny-Wise* (Mar. 1996).

Schook, Florence. Quotation. Ed. Q. David Bowers. *The Numismatist's Downtown Companion, Volume 7.* Wolfeboro, NH: Bowers and Mercena, 1994. 14.

Schwartz, B., Ward, A., Monterosso, J., Lyubomirsky, S., White, K. and Lehman, D. R. "Maximizing Versus Satisficing: Happiness is a Matter of Choice." *Journal of Personality and Social Psychology* 83 (2002): 1178-1197.

Schwartz, S. C. "Narcissism in Collecting Art and Antiques." *Journal of the American Academy of Psychoanalysis* 29 (2001): 633-647.

Sedwick, Daniel and Sedwick, Frank. *The Practical Book of Cobs.* 4th ed. Winter Park, FL: Sedwick, 2007.

Sheldon, William. *Penny Whimsy: A Revision of Early American Cents 1793-1814.* 1958. Lawrence, MA: Quarterman, 1976.

Silvia, P. J. "Interest and Interests: The Psychology of Constructive Capriciousness." *Review of General Psychology* 5 (2001): 270-290.

-----. "What is Interesting? Exploring the Appraisal Structure of Interest." *Emotion* 5 (2005): 89-102.

Stewart, Susan. *On Longing: Narratives of the Miniature, the Gigantic, the Souvenir, and the Collection.* Baltimore, MD: Johns Hopkins University, 1984.

Stone, H. F. "Thrill and Rewards of Ancient Coins." *The Numismatist* 71 (Jan. 1958): 44-45.

Subkowski, Peter. "On the Psychodynamics of Collecting." *International Journal of Psychoanalysis* 87 (2006): 383-401.

Taxay, Don. *The U.S. Mint and Coinage.* New York: Arco, 1969.

The Colonial Coin Collectors Club. www.colonialcoins.org

Todd, F.M. "The Coin Outlasts the Throne." *The Numismatist's Bedside Companion.* Ed. Q. David Bowers. Wolfeboro, NH: Bowers and Merena Galleries, 1987. 33-38.

Travers, Scott. *How to Make Money in Coins Right Now: The Ultimate Insider's Guide to the Coin Market.* New York: Random House, 2001.

-----. *One Minute Coin Expert.* 5th ed. New York: House of Collectibles, 2004.

-----. *The Coin Collector's Survival Manual.* 5th ed. New York: Random House, 2006.

Twain, Mark. The *Adventures of Tom Sawyer.* New York: Harper, 1876.

United States Mint. "Collector's Club: Handling Your Collection." www.usmint.gov n.d. 30 Dec. 2007.

Van Allen, Leroy and Mallis, George. *The Comprehensive Catalogue and Encyclopedia of U.S. Morgan and Peace Silver Dollars.* New York: Arco, 1976.

Van Meter, David. *Collecting Coins & Common Sense: A Complete Survival Guide for Today's Collector and Investor.* Nashua, NH: Laurion Numismatics, 1990.

Volle, E., Beato, R., Levy, R. and Dubois, B. Forced Collectionism after Orbitofrontal Damage. *Neurology* 58 (2002): 488-490.

Wicklund, R. and Gollwitzer, P. *Symbolic Self-Completion.* Hillsdale, NJ: Lawrence Erlbaum, 1982.

Wise, R.A. and Bozarth, M.A. "Brain Mechanisms of Drug Reward and Euphoria." *Psychiatric Medicine* 3 (1985): 445-460.

Wright, John. *The Cent Book: 1816-1839.* Saint Joseph, MI: J. D. Wright, 1992.

Yanchunas, D. "Keeping Collectors on Edge: Adams Dollar Errors Found." *Coinage* (Sep. 2007): 10-11, 14-15.

Yeoman, R. S. ed. *A Guide Book of United States Coins: 2011.* 64th ed. Atlanta: Whitman, 2010.

HAVE MORE FUN & AVOID COSTLY COLLECTING MISTAKES!

Every adventure brings with it the potential for excitement and opportunity to gain new skills, knowledge and confidence, and that couldn't be truer than in collecting coins.

The coin community's very own Answer Man, Alan Herbert, covers all the basics for a sound start in coin collecting, and provides valuable tips and inspiration which are helpful at any phase of your collecting. That's the beauty of the coin collecting adventure, whether you've been collecting for a month or 50 years, new information and new skills are always useful.

In this book the author also takes you inside the mind of some fellow coin collectors, by including intriguing questions he's received over the years, along with his answers. Questions such as:

- **What's the difference between gold leaf and gold foil?**
- **What does an ad mean when it says "a mixed roll of Lincoln cents?"**

- **What is the significance of the dots and dashes around the edge of the Canadian 1943-35 5-cent reverse?**
- **Was President Franklin D. Roosevelt a coin collector?**
- **How did the mint count its coins before the invention of mechanical counting machines?**

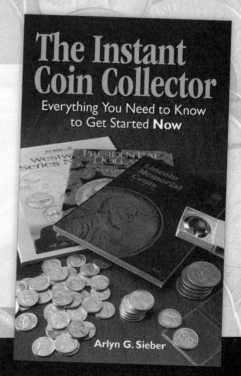

Subscribe Today and Save 61%

Order *Coins* magazine today and you'll get 12 huge issues full of timely information on what and how to collect. You'll see complete coverage of the most important events covering coin collecting, in-depth analyses of market trends, fascinating coin histories, and essential articles to enhance your hobby know-how.

12 ISSUES
GET A FULL YEAR OF

Coins.
FOR JUST
$19.98
plus $3 S&H

SUBSCRIBE ONLINE TODAY

In Canada, add $15 (includes GST/HST). Outside the U.S. and Canada, add $25. Outside the U.S., remit payment in U.S. funds with order. Please allow 4-6 weeks for first-issue delivery. Annual newsstand rate $59.88. *Coins* is published 12 times per year which may include an occasional special, combined or expanded issue that may count as two issues.

TO ORDER, VISIT
subscribe.coinsmagazine.net

Or call 386-246-3421. Or mail orders to Subscription Processing, P.O. Box 420235, Palm Coast FL 32142-0235. Mention offer code J1FHAD